Ethical Glamour and Fashion: Styling Persona Brands

Edited by
Samita Nandy, Kiera Obbard, and Nicole Bojko

WH

WATERHILL
PUBLISHING

ISBN 978-1-7753096-3-5

Contents

Part 1: Fashion in Famous Brands - 'Glamour Labour' in Fame

List of Contributors

Adrian D. Wesołowski is a PhD candidate at Warsaw University, Poland and Max Planck Institute for Social Anthropology in Halle, Germany. Specialised in cultural history and social theory, he strives for a wider adaptation of social sciences methods within the field of history or to historical material. His dissertation investigates the 18th century Europe in order to find the first moments when the themes of philanthropy and fame were inseparably intertwined.

Ana Flora Machado is a PhD fellow in Culture Studies at the School of Human Sciences of the Catholic University of Portugal. She holds a BA degree in Media Studies from Catholic University of Portugal, and an MSc degree in Marketing Management from Aston University Business School, United Kingdom. Her ongoing research is focused on visual gender representations on Social Media, articulating both Media Studies and Visual Culture, her doctoral thesis having the provisional title of 'Selfies on Instagram and the Female Gaze: Digital Performances of Gender Constructions.'

Birte Fritsch is a curator at the Musuem Centre for Persecuted Arts in Solingen. She studied Romance and German Studies, Philosophy and Comparative Literature at the University of Wuppertal. She then undertook doctoral studies at the Graduate School Practices of Literature at the University of Münster. In 2019, she was the curator and project director of the festival Meinwärts. 150 Jahre Else Lasker-Schüler for the Culture Office of the City of Wuppertal.

Bronagh Allison holds a PhD and currently works at the Cognition, Development and Education Research Cluster, Queen's University Belfast. Bronagh does research in Intrapersonal Communications, Experimental Psychology and Evolutionary Psychology, Social Fitness, Creativity and Social Information Exchange. Her current project is 'Gossip and the analaogical peacock'.

Cátia Ferreira holds a PhD in Communication Studies from the Human Sciences School of the Universidade Católica Portuguesa. She is Guest Assistant Professor at FCH-UCP and coordinator of the BA in Social and Cultural Communication and of the Post-Graduate Course in Communication and Content Marketing. She is a senior researcher at the Research Center for Communication and Culture (Universidade Católica Portuguesa), being also part of the Scientific Board, and a researcher at the Centre for Research and Studies in Sociology (ISCTE). Her areas of research and teaching are new media, particularly digital games, social media and mobile devices, multimedia communication, and digital reading practices.

Claudia Ferreira is a PhD candidate at Royal Holloway, University of London. She received an MSc in Politics from the University of Sheffield after earning a BA in Journalism and Public Relations from the University of Porto, Portugal. She has worked in the field of Public Relations for several years in her home country of Portugal. Her research interests include the use of new communication technologies by contemporary social movements.

Douglas Silva is the Dean of the Estácio Juiz de Fora University, Brazil, and a Computer Science professor since 2007. Formerly, he had other senior administrative positions in higher education. From 1999 to 2009 he worked at a software company. He has an undergraduate degree in Computer Science from the CES University (2004), a certificate in Software Process Improvement from the Federal University of Lavras (2006) and a Master of Science Degree in Computer Science from the Federal University of the State of Rio de Janeiro (2012). His main research areas include information systems and social media.

Elliot Pill is a Senior Lecturer at the School of Journalism, Media and Culture at Cardiff University in Wales, UK. He established a successful MA in Global Communication Management in 2001. Mr Pill is the co-author of *Key Concepts in Public Relations* (Sage, 2009) and author of three chapters on Public Relations and Celebrity Culture in *Exploring Public Relations* (Pearson, 2006, 2009, 2014). He also teaches Celebrity Culture at Cardiff University. Before moving into academia, Mr Pill was a newspaper journalist and marketing and public relations consultant. Mr Pill has worked in publicity teams for David Beckham and a range of other celebrities as well as leading international marketing communication campaigns for Lonely Planet, Billabong, Stella Artois, Gillette, Adidas and Pioneer. He has also advised a range of CEO's and organisations on reputation management.

Jaleesa Reed is a Ph.D. Candidate in Polymer, Fiber, and Textile Science with an International Merchandising emphasis. Her research interests revolve around retail, consumers of beauty products, and how women of color navigate retail spaces while negotiating their identity. Her work is interdisciplinary and merges gender studies and human geography with a critical take on fashion consumption. She is the author of *The Beauty Divide: Black Millennial Women*

Seek Agency with Makeup Art Cosmetics (MAC) and *Cosmetic Counter Connotations: Black Millennial Women and Beauty*.

Kabir Bedi is an international actor. His career has spanned three continents covering India, the United States and especially Italy among other European countries in three media: film, television and theatre. Kabir's Italian series *Sandokan* made him a major star across all of Europe. He starred in one of the world's most-watched TV series, *The Bold and Beautiful* and acted in the James Bond *Octopussy*. He has been a voting member of the "Oscars Academy" (Academy of Motion Picture Arts & Sciences) since 1982. He has recently received an Honorary Doctorate from Kalinga Institute of Industrial Technology (KIIT), India.

Katalin Medvedev holds a PhD and is an international dress and fashion scholar. Her ongoing research interests focus on the construction and expression of cultural identity through dress, gender and the politics of dress, fashion and empowerment, fashion peripheries, and fashion and sustainability. Her latest large project was editing a book titled *Dress and Empowerment* for Bloomsbury Publishing. Currently, she explores diversity issues with her Ph.D. students in the fashion industrial complex. Topics include the analysis of Corporate Social Responsibility initiatives that focus on racial injustice, racialized beauty retail environments, and ageism in the fashion industry. In addition, we are developing a course on fashion and diversity that furthers both fashion and general education.

Kiera Obbard is a PhD student in Literary Studies, School of English and Theatre Studies at the University of Guelph in Ontario, Canada. Her current research is situated at the intersection of contemporary Canadian poetry, technology, and digital humanities. She completed her M.A. in Cultural Studies and Critical theory at McMaster University and her Honours B.A. with a joint major in English and Communication at the University of Ottawa. She is currently a fellow at The Humanities Interdisciplinary Collaboration (THINC) Lab, an editorial board member of the Centre for Media and Celebrity Studies and WaterHill Publishing, and she works full-time at the Waterloo-based software company OpenText.

Lindsay Parker holds an MA in Fashion Cultures from London College of Fashion where her research focused on the use of, and discourse surrounding, furs and plumage in fashion. Prior to this, she earned a BA Hons in Fashion (Footwear and Accessories) from Northampton University and has taught for several years in further education. She is currently working towards a PhD in Culture, Media and the Creative Industries at King's College, London where her research is centred on contemporary approaches to more sustainable modes of fashion consumption.

Lori Hall-Araujo teaches in the Fashion Program at Stephens College in Columbia, Missouri, USA where she is also Curator for the Costume Museum and Research Library. She is currently completing the monograph *The Missing Body from the Carmen Miranda Museum*, which revisits field research in Brazil, reflects on her own Latinx identity, and addresses the implications of communication via the body, dress, and performance. Among her other publications are contributions to the forthcoming *Bloomsbury Encyclopedia of Film Costume*.

Luis Fernando Romo was born in Barcelona (Spain). In 2017 he earned his Ph.D. in Media, Communication, and Culture at the Universitat Autònoma of Barcelona (UAB). His research on rumors and celebrities in the Spanish gossip magazines explores in what way famous people are positioned and empowered by the use of rumor built as a narrative. His scholarly interest focus on the intersections of celebrity (capital), identity, glamour, and rumors. Throughout his professional career as a freelance journalist, he has worked for Hearst Publishers, Playboy, La Vanguardia, El Mundo, and the Big Five Spanish gossip magazines: Lecturas, Semana, ¡Hola!, Diez Minutos and Pronto. On the internet, he has collaborated for El Español, WorlOnline/Tiscali, and Wowowow.com, created by Liz Smith, the Grand Dame of Gossip in New York. In television, he has been a freelancer for Telecinco, Divinity, TV3, and 8Tv and in radio for RNE. He has been visiting professor at UAB and ESERP Business School and has been a speaker in Brussels, Barcelona, and Lisbon.

Maria Murumaa-Mengel is a PhD in media and communication, is a social media lecturer and the program director of journalism and communication studies at the Institute of Social Studies, University of Tartu. She is involved in research focusing mainly on young people's use (and non-use, going "off the grid") of social media, digital literacies (social media literacies and porn literacies) and the transformation of private and public in online spaces. More specifically, her most recent research has looked into how young people construct and navigate the online-intimate (e.g. Tinder and online-pornography), how online risks (e.g. digital shaming, "online perverts") and opportunities (e.g. microcelebrity, online communities) are changing everyday practices of youth. Furthermore, Maria is interested in the methodological aspects of creative (online) research methods and the ethical considerations in studying sensitive topics.

Maureen Lehto Brewster is a doctoral student in International Merchandising at the University of Georgia. She previously earned a master's degree in Fashion Studies from Parsons School of Design. Her research interests include celebrity and influencer culture, social media, gender, and the body. Her writing has appeared in *The International Journal of Fashion Studies*; *Fashion, Style and Popular Culture*; *Journal of Design and Culture*, and *The Iconic*. Maureen has also been featured on Buzzfeed News, The Business of Fashion, and Women's Wear Daily. You can follow her work on Instagram at @soldbycelebs.

Nicole Bojko holds a Ph.D. in French Language and Literature from the State University of New York at Buffalo. She specializes in the spatial poetics of existentialist literature and Quebec studies. A New Hampshire native, she currently lives in California where she spends her time raising her two young sons as well as teaching French language courses at Cerro Coso Community College. Dr. Bojko enjoys existential conversations, practicing yoga, hiking with her family, and watching Formula 1 racing.

Nikki Soo is a postdoctoral research associate at Cardiff University's School of Journalism, Media, and Culture, working on an AHRC-funded project 'Countering Disinformation: Enhancing journalistic legitimacy in public service media'. Her research focuses on political communication and public policy, specifically the integration and impact of digital technology in society, media and culture. Read more about her work at www.nikkisoo.com or www.twitter.com/sniksw.

Olga Andreevskikh is a London-based PhD candidate at the School of Languages, Cultures and Societies of the University of Leeds (thesis title: "Constructing LGBTQ identities: Russian media in the context of the 'traditional sexuality' legislation"). Before coming to the UK for the PhD programme in 2015, Olga had spent over 10 years working as an assistant professor at the Nizhny Novgorod State Linguistics University (Nizhny Novgorod, Russia), teaching Russian and English as foreign languages. She holds a PhD degree in English literature and a Bachelor's degree in Russian, English and Literary Studies.

Patrick Nogly is currently an MA Student in Philosophy and Hispanic Studies at the University of Wuppertal. He obtained his bachelor's degree with work on Spanish naturalist writer Emilia Pardo Bazán. At the moment, he is finishing his master's thesis on the Spanish poet Federico García Lorca and the influences of the platonic philosophy of love in his work The Public. Additionally, since 2017 he has been working as a freelance texter for several companies.

Pete Sigal is professor of History and Gender, Sexuality and Feminist Studies at Duke University and president of the American Society for Ethnohistory. He is author of *The Flower and the Scorpion: Sexuality and Ritual in Early Nahua Culture* (Duke University Press, 2011), a study of sexual representation in sixteenth and seventeenth-century indigenous Nahua societies of Mexico, which won the Erminie Wheeler Voegelin Award from the American Society of Ethnohistory. He is co-editor, with Zeb Tortorici and the late Neil Whitehead, of *Ethnopornography: Sexuality, Colonialism and Archival Knowledge* (Duke University Press, 2020), a study of the relationships between the colonial and ethnographic gaze and sexuality throughout the world. He is currently completing a study of colonialism and sexual desire, "Sustaining Sexual Pleasure: A History of Colonial and Postcolonial Voyeurism." Sigal also is author of *From Moon Goddesses to Virgins: The Colonization of Yucatecan Maya Sexual Desire* (University of Texas, 2000), and editor of *Infamous Desire: Male Homosexuality in Colonial Latin America* (University of Chicago Press, 2003).

Piia Õunpuu is a communication and marketing consultant. She has a Master's degree in Communication Management from the Institute of Social Studies, University of Tartu. Her main academic and professional interest lies in social media celebrities and influencers, her research is mainly related the different ethical viewpoints of influencers' self-presentation and advertising practices. As a micro-influencer herself, she has participated in the local blogosphere since 2010 and in her research, has an additional insider researcher view. She is currently working closely with the relevant authorities and other industry experts on developing an official guide of conduct for Estonian microinfluencers. Piia's research for the current chapter was supported by Archimedes Foundation and the Dora Pluss grant.

Renata Prado is a Brazilian professor, journalist and designer. She has been awarded a Doctorate in Technologies of Communication from the Department of Media at Universidade do Estado do Rio de Janeiro, Brazil. Her PhD dissertation "Books and Readers on YouTube's Sociability Networks" analyze how literary YouTube channels known as *booktube* communicate reading experiences and affections towards books. Renata's works investigate uses and appropriations of social media, especially with regard to readers and books on these communication platforms. She is also interested in topics such as fan culture, game studies, celebrities and media history. She teaches Digital Media and Editorial Design at Estacio Juiz de Fora for Journalism, Advertising, Graphic Design and Fashion Design graduate students.

Samita Nandy is an author and cultural critic of fame. She holds a Doctorate in celebrity culture from the Department of Media & Information at Curtin University, Australia and is a certified broadcast journalist from Canada. As the Director of Centre for Media and Celebrity Studies (CMCS), Samita Nandy Productions, and author of *Becoming Media Critics* and *Fame in Hollywood North*, Nandy is the first celebrity studies scholar to be on tabloid and has been publicized for her views in media, including The Telegraph (UK), CBC, VICE, Flare, Chatelaine, SUN Media, 24 Hrs news Yahoo! Entertainment and many more. She has been published in *Celebrity Studies* and in a number of book chapters.

Vehbi Gorgulu is an Assistant Professor at the Department of Communication Design and Management, Head of Public Relations Department and the Director of Public Relations and Corporate Communication MA program at Istanbul Bilgi University.

Vitor Sérgio Ferreira has a Ph.D. in Sociology. He is currently Research Fellow at the Instituto de Ciências Sociais, Universidade de Lisboa, where he is the head of the research group LIFE—Life Course, Inequalities and Solidarities: Practices and Policies. His research interests include issues of youth cultures and its bodily expressions, new aspirational labour and youth transitions to labour market, and generational change and inequality. Among his recent publications are the following: Youth and generations in times of crisis: Portugal in the global situation (2018). In Lobo, Silva and Zúquete (eds.). *Changing Societies: Legacies and Challenges. Citizenship in Crisis*, Lisbon: Imprensa de Ciências Sociais, pp. 135-160; Being a DJ is not just pressing the Play: the pedagogization of a new dream job (2017). *Revista Educação & Realidade,* 42 (20), pp. 473-494; Aesthetics of youth scenes: from arts of resistance to arts of existence (2016). *Young - Nordic Journal of Youth Research*, 24 (1), pp. 66-81.

Victoria Kannen writes and teaches on the subjects of identity, privilege, education, and popular culture. She holds a PhD in Sociology and Equity Studies in Education from the Ontario Institute for Studies in Education at the University of Toronto. Victoria is the co-editor of *The Spaces and Places of Canadian Popular Culture* (Canadian Scholars Press, 2019). Her work has also been published in such journals as the *Journal of Gender Studies, Culture, Theory and Critique*, and *Teaching in Higher Education.*

Foreword

Where is Ethical Glamour in Celebrity Culture?

Elliot Pill

The global fashion industry is central to the cultural production of celebrities as brands. The cultural spaces of the runway, the international fashion weeks, and the mediation of 'seasonal' looks, have been appropriated by both celebrities and associated cultural intermediaries to form opinions, amplify ideas, and create systems of economic exchange.

Further, if we define Celebrity Culture to mean, "collections of sense making practices whose main resource of meaning are celebrities" (Driessens, 2014), and take a Hofstedeian position that, "culture is the collective programming of the mind which distinguished one category of people from another" (Hofstede, 1984), we begin to see the academic necessity in debating, dissecting, and critiquing pressing issues related to the ethical processes used by celebrities in forming personas of glamour in these 'fashion' spaces.

So, as citizens, fans, followers, and likers make sense of the world around them through the projection of celebrity lives in these fashion spaces and associated practices of modeling, it is time to set the pause button. It is time to dim the promotional noise switch and deflate the balloon carrying the oxygen of publicity, to consider the ways in which celebrities use, and in growing ways, abuse the current opiate of the masses – attention.

In this light, I am delighted that the problems of ethics in relation to the glamorizing processes used by celebrities and their cultural intermediaries are being raised and questioned in this publication. You will see, in the following publication, selected edited and peer reviewed papers, rich in material investigations, into the diverse issues related to ethical glamour and celebrity culture.

Three specific areas are investigated with a wide-ranging selection of thought-provoking research comprising: Fashion in Persona Brands; Styles in Ethical Influencer Marketing and Brand Promotion and Eco Models and Role Models in Celebrity Culture. The papers are global in nature and explore issues such as race, gender, class, poverty and shame. Themes of research include fashion capital; transitions from glory to fame; representation and transmedia, and DIY content, analyzing the celebrity personas of, among others, Meghan Markle, Robert Mapplethorpe, Rihanna, Emma Watson, and Bibi Russell.

Indeed, we could perhaps be at a tipping point where these issues and debates become everyday discussions leading to policy changes with the realization of Aeron Davis' research of a promotionally saturated world:

> Promotion appears everywhere, so much so that we no longer notice… It is common to ask questions about how finance, globalization, digital technologies and war shape our world, but no-one asks much about our promotion-saturated world. (Davis, 2013)

So, as we are challenging the effects of this promotionally saturated world and analyzing the way, in this specific context, celebrities use glamorizing systems to extend and re-represent personas, let me first unpack some issues rendering this subject field so important, before moving on to give some examples of unethical and damaging campaigns run by celebrities to sustain their brand.

Professor Stephen Powis, a medical director of the United Kingdom's National Health Service, argues that celebrity-led social media advertising campaigns, marketing weight loss aids, should be banned as they have such a damaging effect on the physical and mental health of young people. He urged celebrities to act more responsibly in the choice of products they chose to promote, citing an example of Kim Kardashian's short-lived promotion of two weight loss products. The first was an appetite-suppressing lollypop and the second was a meal replacement shake created by flattummeyco.

These unregulated adverts targeted her 126 million Instagram followers where 3 million followers and fans engaged with the content by liking the promotional posts related to both products. Actress and body positive campaigner, Jameela Jamil, labeled the Kardashian campaigns as 'terrible' with a 'toxic' influence on young girls.

Indeed, the social influencer space and regulation is such a contested issue that in the UK, The Competition and Markets Authority (CMA), has warned celebrities that they will be fined if they continue to fail to let audiences know products and services they promote are indeed, adverts. Celebrities found promoting products without making fans aware were, among others, Ellie Goulding, Rita Ora, and models, Alexa Chung and Rosie Huntingdon-Whiteley.

Another example of where fashion, modeling and the runway are used in a subliminal and ethically questionable way is offered in an analysis of Formula One racing celebrity, Lewis Hamilton. Hamilton, a five-time world Formula One (F1) racing driver, is widely regarded as the finest drivers of his generation and the fastest driver ever to have driven in F1. The first black F1 racing driver, he uses an array of social media platforms to influence fans and connect brand messages to his audiences from sponsors such as fashion brands, Puma and

Tommy Hilfiger. To extend his celebrity persona outside of F1, Hamilton uses his body, as both a cultural site and a site for economic exchange. He launched a clothing range with Tommy Hilfiger last year; created a series of 'hamojis' to digitize his persona; storified his extensive tattoos in a range of media interviews in Men's Health and took to the cover of GQ magazine wearing a tartan kilt in order to address criticism of him gender shaming his nephew during a social media video carried on his Instagram feed. In one promotion, Hamilton asked his 3.8 million Instagram followers to come up with design ideas for his next racing helmet for the 2017 season. 8,000 design ideas were submitted and many lines of editorial publicity were created in debating the competition and subsequent designs and winning results. Hamilton, gaining vast sums of free editorial coverage, announced the winning design, on his own Instagram platform, as that submitted by professional graphic designer, Rai Caldato. The odds seemed a little fixed against the fan in winning this competition.

An example of unethical promotion is related to Storm model, Cara Delevigne. In 2017, Delevigne, who has 36.4 million Instagram followers, was paid to promote a tropical island as a new holiday destination. The whole island was given to her and her friends for free so long as they promoted each day via their social media followers. Neither Delevigne, nor any of her party, told any of their fans that they were, in fact, acting on behalf of the island's owners and their related social media posts were therefore commercial adverts.

These examples, and the many more illuminating papers you are about to read, signify a seminal point in the academic study of celebrities, the spaces in which they shape and present their personas and the tactics they use to inflate their ever-growing bubbles of publicity.

The study of such subjects is important because much has been written, researched, and theorized in relation to media and advertising literacy, but little has been written related to a broader academic analysis of promotional literacy. This understanding would allow audiences to understand the way in which their social media lives and subsequent actions are subliminally manipulated with exposure to unregulated promotional and advertising campaigns featuring the famous, infamous, and influential.

Dr. Elliot Pill

School of Journalism, Media and Culture
Cardiff University, Wales, UK

References

Driessens, O. (2014) Theorizing celebrity cultures: thickenings of celebrity cultures and the role of cultural (working) memory. *Communications: European Journal of Communication Research*, 39 (2). pp. 109-127.

Davis, A. (2013). Living in 'promotional times'. openDemocracy, 14 June 2013. https://www.opendemocracy.net/en/opendemocracyuk/living-in-promotional-times/. Accessed March 17, 2020.

Ellen MacArthur Foundation *(2019). A New Textiles Economy: Redesigning Fashion's Future*, November 2019. https://www.gov.uk/government/news/celebrities-pledge-to-clean-up-their-act-on-social-media. Accessed March 27th, 2019.

Hofstede, G. (1984). National cultures and corporate cultures. In L.A. Samovar & R.E. Porter (Eds.), *Communication Between Cultures*. Belmont, CA: Wadsworth.

Ives, L (2019). Celebrity ads for diet aids should be banned, says top doctor; https://www.bbc.co.uk/news/health-47090374

Introduction to *Ethical Glamour and Fashion: Styling Persona Brands*

Samita Nandy, Kiera Obbard, and Nicole Bojko

Celebrity culture and the notion of "model" in fame have transformed dramatically with the pervasiveness and ubiquity of social media. Whereas these spheres of influence have traditionally required actual, physical objects and spaces, such as studios, headshots, audition tapes, and financial investments, social media platforms are now able to transcend these material conditions; they facilitate communication and network building between individuals (and organizations) who traditionally might be unable to connect due to location, fiscal burden or a host of other such limiting factors. They equally give rise to aesthetic communication, such as visual storytelling, which is a powerful tool in the ethical use of glamour in modeling.

This current book project arises from the Centre for Media and Celebrity Studies' 7th international conference Bridging Gaps: Where is Ethical Glamour in Celebrity Culture? in Lisbon, which problematized what it meant to be a "model" and addressed the larger question of Where is Ethical Glamour in Celebrity Culture? The fashion modeling industry has occupied a significant area in celebrity culture. For the past four decades, popular models, actors, authors, academics, and athletes among many public figures have had the ability to stylize their profile pictures and build their persona brand through visual and literary expressions of fashion. As a part of their aesthetic communication of stories, these expressions of fashion have successfully played a key role in publicity and promotion of their ethical brands. But are all persona brands authentic and ethical? If so, how can we construct and popularize persona brands for a social cause? For the purpose of this edited collection, we need to first understand how a brand can be defined in aesthetic communication of fashion and, more importantly, in style for recognizing ethical role models.

Defining Persona Brand

In defining a persona brand, we need to understand the concept of brand and how it might be meaningfully applied to the context of persona studies. A brand is a metaphor (Davies and Chun, 2003), an entity located within human intuitive ontology as an artefact (e.g. see De Cruz and De Smedt, 2007). The concept of a brand has been extended to identifying public figures and not just their commercial products or services. In this respect, personal brand is a commercial identity that consists of one's "biography, experience, skills, behaviours, appearance and your name" (Gander 2014). A persona is an identity used to articulate a personal brand— a combination of selected personality traits, reputation, national identity, and many more social identifiers. It has its etymological origins in the Latin word "mask," which points towards its performative nature. Erving Goffman's dramaturgical approach sheds light on the persona as a performance of a mediated self in everyday life (1959). For Goffman, people use narratological and symbolic mechanisms to perform public selves during social interactions. As in theatre, the performed self is not necessarily real, but based on perceptions of what may constitute as real during the social interactions.

David Marshall (2015) extends the performance of self to understanding persona as a public identity that holds a strategic and negotiated agency. In this perspective, a persona brand is an identity that may or may not lead to commercial exchange but can act as cultural capital/asset embodying affective values in its symbolic expressions (Nandy, 2015). Expressions and substitutes of the persona, such as creations of artists in the form of artwork and activism, hold brand value whereby the brand is a "differentiating mark" and "value indicator" (Wheaton and Nandy, 2015). Persona brands then reflect and reinforce artistic possibilities to explore individual experience—for example, stylistic possibilities that are intricately tied to one's ethical stance in fashion, glamour, and overall aesthetic communication. As seen in the chapters of this collection, implementation of ethical understandings and practices of the persona brand – alongside marketing communication - can lead to similar impacts of celebrity activism while lessening the risk of the brand's devaluation that is often an unfortunate experience for celebrity activists subject to tabloid narratives such as gossip, rumor, and scandals for fan consumption.

For fans, celebrities become "role models" who help construct subjectivity and become objects of study, especially when it comes to the consumption of beauty ideals and sexual objectification of the body. Indeed, sexual and other forms of scandal can devalue a persona constructed around ideals. Therefore, as seen in fame, the value of celebrity indexical substitutes (e.g., artistic expression of personas) has the capacity to decrease, despite their traditional Marxist values remaining the same in moments of scandal, gossip, and rumors (Wheaton and Nandy, 2019). At the same time, the value of activist art can increase if complex yet authentic elements of storytelling can be restored in celebrity persona. Social causes such as human rights, animal rights, and environmental sustainability, and the conditions under which they restored, are indeed complex. By examining indexical substitutes using persona, affect-value, and Marxist theory, we might resolve celebrity scandal devaluing and identify how affective parts of celebrity activism may be reclaimed using contextual elements of biographies in visual storytelling and its sensory aesthetics (Wheaton and Nandy, 2019). We ask: instead of simply following celebrity narratives, can fans critically study and use narrative structures in celebrity persona and become new role models, making their ethical cause famous in celebrity activism?

As displays of online personas become increasingly prolific in social media, these online personas may or may not have commercial exchange in fame yet assume similar cultural capital in fandom. The construction of such personas has the capacity to engage with aesthetics and politics of celebrity activism – the will to act using fame-based understandings. While selected personal traits are not far from the human behaviors, the gap between persona and self is widening in online celebrity culture. This gap calls for restoring authenticity that can be both reflected and resolved by diverse communication that challenges class-based biopolitics in gendered, racialized, and gendered spaces. Thus, to achieve success in social change, the pedagogical and scholarly value of persona is invaluable, in that it demands ethical and symbolic understanding of persona brands in higher education. On one hand, we are seeking to teach people about persona so that they can critically engage. On the other, we are seeking to develop an improved understanding of persona through scholarly study to help answer ethical questions.

Despite the prominence of higher education, legal policies, and availability of useful online information, there is continuity of "lookism" in the discrimination of sex, race, class, and species, as well as other marginalized categories. For Louis Tietje Steven Cresap, lookism describes prejudice toward people because of their appearance (2005). While words can lead to progressive thoughts, they also have the capacity for categorization and discrimination. This discrimination illustrates that words can fail. Moreover, while rationality has opened the door for progressive thinking, it has also enabled greater categorization and discrimination. Nonetheless, celebrity activists and everyday life role models are using authentic ways of visual storytelling, for example, displays of ethical fashion, to help others bring positive change. They refashion stories and inspire fans, students, and scholars to become role models in the process. The success then lies not in the combination of visual and literary expressions of 'fashion' but in the 'style' in which role models offer a voice. The voice in 'styles' of literal and visual communication (as in the authenticity of storytelling for social change) informs current practices on developing ethical influencer marketing and sustainability over power structures that sustain profit-driven egos.

In light of the 'style' of eco-centric voice over ego-centric 'fashion', we further ask: How can we use academic study and cultural productions to expand traditional definitions and understandings of modeling? Can the body become a biological tool to re-fashion dominant notions of glamour? Would the use of the body include voices of diverse abilities and, in the process, contest ableism, lookism, and speciesism in ethical fashion and glamour? Can the skin, as in the case of PETA nudists, become a particular text and be semiotically read in a way that accepts, negotiates, or disrupts what it means to be a green glamour model in celebrity culture? Can newly defined green glamour models lead to much needed liberal and democratic practices in celebrity activism and studies of celebrity culture? The book addresses if exploitative labor is sustainable from the perspective of social and environmental ethics. Despite ethical issues, is sustainable and ethical use of glamourous fashion foreseeable? The book recognizes celebrities as examples for new role models to mobilize glamour in ways that can partly or wholly facilitate environmentally sustainable glamour that includes visual representation of diverse ethnic looks, fair trade labor, and cruelty-free clothes with no leather, fur silk and wool among other non-human byproducts. The book shows a sustainable solution in the visual storytelling of such fashion unfolds in a complex but progressive manner.

The following chapters explore the complex and multifaceted nature of this question through a combination of theoretical and methodological perspectives in three sections. These foundational studies shed particular light on a variety of themes including poverty, race, gender, shame, and the social function of fame. While the individual chapters themselves deal with specific aspects relating to celebrity culture, notions of presence, space, and visibility emerge as underlying and unifying themes of the larger project divided under the following three parts: 1) Fashion in Persona Brands, 2) Styles in Ethical Influencer Marketing, and 3) Eco-Models.

Part 1. Fashion in Persona Brands - The Problem of "Glamour Labor" in Fame

Art and its cultural consumption, according to Pierre Bourdieu, are predisposed to the communication of legitimatized social distinctions. For Rebecca Halliday (2016), Bourdieu's concept of the "field of cultural production" particularly describes "fashion's industrial structures and members' accumulation, investment and display of economic and cultural capital" (p. 21). Extending the concept of cultural capital, Entwistle and Rocamora (2006) articulate what they refer to as "fashion capital," or a type of cultural capital that is specific to the fashion industry. Halliday (2016) explains that fashion capital is "embodied and indeed performed via social practices, the wearing of fashionable clothes and the maintenance of one's physical appearance." When celebrity personas become connected to the fashion industry, they employ their fashion capital to influence consumer fashion choices and buying patterns. Importantly, celebrity's fashion persona must also be aligned to their existing persona to be effective. Through clothing choices, photographs, interviews, and social media postings, celebrities perform their fashion persona to influence the public in ethically sustainable fashion practices. In this way, fashion becomes an aesthetic communication tool that celebrities use to articulate distinctions in ethically sustainable fashion and glamour. For Elizabeth Wissinger, however, the "glamour labor" involved in self-fashioning, surveillance, and branding is often an inevitable and unfortunate outcome in the production of consumer values and desirable bodies. If fashion functions to communicate social distinctions, it risks reinforcing class, race, and gender hierarchies and loses its material and symbolic role in restoring heroic efforts in fame. The rising interest in critical studies of fame carries investments in intellectual labor that, on one hand, meets commodified needs of understanding analytical terms. The increase in intellectual labor, on another hand, limits physical effort in extending and applying analysis for the social change it envisions.

In the opening chapter, "No more than a brand. Debating Lilti on glory essentialism", Adrian Wesolowski offers his theoretical and methodological insight into restoring the concept of role models in celebrity studies. Using a historical approach, Wesolowski particularly conceptualizes the process of transition from "glory-recognition" to "fame-recognition" as an ethical way to establish modern models. Glory, as in the case of Mother Theresa and many other famous philanthropists, has led to consider them as role models, but the lack of defining it as a form of fame risks undertaking studies and practices of celebrity culture as superficial. Wesolowski suggests further researching glory as two other foundational themes – commemoration and aspiration in fame.

While Wesolowski looks at restoring role models in historical and contemporary contexts of celebrity studies, Lori Hall-Araujo looks at the pedagogical value of using specific media research methods and research-framing theories in examining ideological understandings of beauty and glamour in celebrity culture. She looks at the use of social media among American female college students that practitioners and scholars can critically consider in their ethical explorations of persona branding on a global level.

The ideological way in which beauty and glamour is used is not limited to the persona branding of women. The way Robert Mapplethorpe's positioned and promoted himself as a celebrity photographer is well illustrated in Pete Sigal's chapter "The Model as (Black) Phallus: Milton Moore, Thomas

Williams, and Robert Mapplethorpe." Mapplethorpe appears to represent Black men in a way that is desirable and popular – his advertisement with model Milton Moore inverts the position of Thomas Williams. However, his exotic and questionable way of 'Othering' race and practicing speciesism in the unsustainable use of leather shows that the progress of ethical glamour and sustainable fashion, in general, is complex.

The complexity of representing equality in popular practices of branding is observed in mediated representation of sexuality. In her case study of the TV show "Fashion Sentence", Olga Andreevskikh shows the use of celebrity brand gestures as a part of fashionable style. She particularly shows how this gestural communication mediates non-heteronormative sexuality and gender performance while reinforcing the state-imposed discourse of traditional sexual norms.

Bronagh Allison looks beyond the mere production level of celebrity brands. Since fame is a complex interplay of media, government, businesses, and fan participation, her examination of the social function of gossip is useful in assessing complex realities of an ethical celebrity. In "Gossip and persona: Online gossip and perceptions of Meghan Markle's identity work", she offers a case study of an article on Celebitchy.com that illustrates the challenges that role models face in the stylistic performance of their persona.

At the same time, Lindsay Parker's "The Role of Celebrity in the Fur Debate" envisions promise for ethical style and fashion despite imperfections within and beyond celebrity culture. Her chapter explores the powerful impact which celebrity personas have in the promotion of fur as well as supporters of anti-fur campaigns. The dual and complex role of personal branding in the structuring of arguments for and against the unsustainable material shows how the ethical use of marketing skills can reflect wider progressive attitudes. Celebrities' sustainable lifestyle could be increasingly used to promote anti-fur sentiment in the near future. More importantly, fans can use similar skills in becoming role models in using ethical influencer marketing to lessen carbon footprints, promote fair trade, and biodiversity.

Part 2. Styles in Ethical Influencer Marketing - Brand Promotion

In promoting influential brands, we need ethical practices that address not only diversity and inclusion, but also other ethical considerations such as eco-fashion and sustainability. As Rebecca Oxford suggests, sustainability not only supports human beings but all other species in our ecosystem. Therefore, the idea of modeling in contemporary practices of eco-fashion intends to reflect care towards the quality of all life, respect human rights, promote biodiversity, and bring balance among all species. A diverse range of celebrities employs their fashionable personas in their modeling practices to influence sustainable eco-fashion. Such modeling should be inclusive of all shapes, postures, and voices while promoting eco-fashion in diverse sectors of work and leisure. Beauty entrepreneurs like Rihanna use their celebrity personas to launch beauty lines that advocate for and provide visibility to women of color in the beauty industry. Similarly, Bibi Russell has transformed her celebrity capital as supermodel into a fashion designer brand to promote ethically sustainable collections and ecological consciousness among diverse ethnic looks in the industry. Such changes in the fashion industry have led to transformations in the forms of embodiment deemed acceptable in the modeling industry. This democratization of models' appearance and diversification of body types welcomed in the industry represents activism for new ethical values of inclusion and diversity in addition to using sustainable wear.

Social media also plays a pivotal role in how celebrities tell stories and mobilize their personas and brand to endorse, support, and promote activist causes. Celebrities use transmedia logics and strategies to share their brand and communicate more ethical messages. From the #timesup movement to the fur debate, Facebook, Instagram, and Twitter have all been used by celebrities in recent years to promote and drive activist causes. Dominant ideologies shared on social media platforms inform cultural use of certain forms of fashion, makeup, and beauty products. At the same time, representations of celebrity fashion, style, and bodies on social media provide opportunities for the body to become a site of resistance to white-centric beauty ideals. Thus, celebrity activism circulated through social media has the potential to endorse activist causes, critique idealized systems of beauty and fashion, drive social movements, and enable collective social change. Fans can also become known as (role) models for mobilizing and empowering the public in a way that is independent of biased and unsustainable practices in traditional media and other institutions. The knowledge and practice of the required skills in becoming such models can be considered in the following chapters.

In "Transmedia, branding and celebrities," Cátia Ferreira and Ana Flora Machado show how transmedia logics and strategies can be extended to branded content production in celebrity culture. Vehbi Gorgulu shows how the production, distribution, and reception of allure is not glamorous. In his chapter "Not that glam: Marketing in DIY fashion and #TFWGucci meme campaign," Gorgulu shows the structured use of collaborative memetic marketing. The meaning-making processes of #TFWGucci campaign helps us to understand how ethical goals can be effectively achieved with the transformative digital content creation and marketing practices.

The influential role of transmedia in creating famous brands such as that of the Kardashians and Gucci can be applied to ethical causes; however, the social responsibility of embracing ethics does not depend on their producers of fame. In the chapter "Estonian fashion/beauty bloggers' practices and ethical dilemmas in featuring branded and sponsored content", Maria Murumaa-Mengel and Piia Ounpuu point out ethical dilemmas that beauty and fashion bloggers face when featuring sponsored posts on their blogs. While the Kardashians appear to be role models for positing themselves as social media influencers and agents of change, most influencers lack the know-how and resources to develop and enforce any formal regulations in their own content production practices. The emergence of vague self-regulating principles illustrates that the onus is on the audience, and just producers, to develop ethical practices for decoding beauty content in influencer marketing.

"Is an ethics of bodily inclusion emerging in the glamorous world of fashion models?" The rhetorical question in Vitor Sérgio Ferreira's book chapter shows actual progress in the democratization of the models' appearance and audience acceptance of the models. In his interviews with professional fashion bookers and young fashion models, Ferreira particularly shows how diversification of corporeality in modeling is being welcomed in the fashion market. The structural changes in the fashion industry enable a new ethics of inclusive forms of embodiment and recognizing worth in diverse bodily capital.

One of the ways to effectuate structural change is by not depending on traditional producers. Rather, aspiring and established models and other performance artists become cultural producers of living examples of change and content they wish to see. In her chapter, "Beauty Entrepreneur with Social Conscience: Rihanna Gets Real with her Power and Influence," Jaleesa Reed and Katalin Medvedev show how the superstar has used her entrepreneurial skills to venture into fashion, philanthropy, diplomacy, and beauty. The way in which she intertwines her persona with her product is an example for models and fashion producers to advocate for visibility and voice for women of color in the beauty industry.

For Victoria Kannen, social media has helped with democratizing beauty practices in celebrity culture. In her chapter, "Snooki has #noshame: Representations and Redefinitions of Celebrity, Beauty, and Empowerment on Instagram," famous figures such as Nicole Polizzi have begun to flaunt the ways in which bodies are modified. In the process, they become role models mobilizing dialogues resisting shame and exoticization of what used to be hidden earlier. In the process, they position the body as an ethical site for potential resistance to white-centric beauty ideals and reclamation of the self beyond learned behaviors of idealized Western beauty.

Part 3. Eco-Models - Role Models in Celebrity Culture

Are progressive thoughts towards ethical acts in modeling necessarily eco-friendly? Fair trade fashion is significant but, for this purpose, the practice of re-styling models and portraying diverse, eco-role models is about further navigating the contested spaces of glamour production. The exploitative use of non-unionized human labor and bodies, animal skin and fur, fossil fuel, and emission of polluting agents in the garment industry and slaughterhouses, producing by-products such as leather and wool, prompts us to redefine what it means to be an eco-model as opposed to a high fashion role model that once excluded diverse bodies. Celebrities like Emma Watson use their persona on social media to promote sustainable fashion and style and effectively brand themselves as models (both as a fashion model and a model to follow) of ethical glamour in the sustainable fashion community. Famous PETA models use their cultural capital to question anti-fur production and mobilize public opinion on what it means to engage in ethical fashion.

With the ever-increasing presence of social media in our lives, influencer marketing and advertisements have become integral components of global popular culture and the fashion industry. Celebrities and beauty bloggers collaborate with fashion designers and luxury brands to celebritize products and services and create fandom on social media, which raises certain ethical questions and dilemmas regarding the practice of ethical influencer marketing. Nevertheless, celebrity activism within and beyond Hollywood re-stylizes examples of ethical role models that can consider using online media.

In her chapter, "Emma Watson's 'The Press Tour': Fashion Activism as Personal Brand," author Maureen Brewster shows the critical role of personal brand in celebrity activism. The author particularly shows how actress and activist Emma Watson branded herself as a model of an ethical fashionista in sustainable fashion to mobilize a connective action network. For this purpose, Emma Watson pledged to wear only sustainably produced green clothing as a part of her aesthetic communication for press appearances in 2015. This chapter offers a discursive analysis of her Instagram account, "The Press Tour" that she started in 2017 to document her sustainable style in Hollywood.

In Hollywood, where sexual objectification and abuse have been part of patriarchal practices of glamour production, celebrity activism has shifted from personal to collective action. In their chapter, "Reframing Hollywood: Dissecting the celebrity-led #timesup initiative," authors Claudia Ferreira and Nikki Soo show how, unlike typical celebrity activism, celebrities are the driving force behind political actions against misogynistic behavior by beloved entertainment personalities, such as Harvey Weinstein. The authors focus on the 2018 Golden Globes, where celebrity activism was prioritized over patriarchal forms of glamour and mobilized activism on social media. The chapter particularly shows how celebrity tweets with the hashtag #timesup re-brand celebrities as forces for social change rather than endorsing causes for profitable reasons. As opposed to past celebrity endorsements, role models in post-Weinstein era of celebrity activism can result in widespread connective and collective action for ethical glamour.

The rhetorical question in the chapter "How Can a Supermodel Influence Social, Environmental and Animal Causes through Social Media? A Case Study with the Brazilian Supermodel Gisele Bündchen" shows complex yet progressive directions that social media enabled in celebrity activism. Here authors Douglas Silva and Renata Silva use quantitative methods to show how celebrity activism is effectively used in resisting animal and environmental exploitation in glamorous fashion. Using the case study of Gisele Bündchen, the authors concluded that the followers are not primarily interested in her activism posts but engage with her persona endorsing the cause beyond Hollywood.

While Brazilian supermodel Gisele Bündchen endorses animal and environmental ethics, Bangladeshi supermodel Bibi Russell uses her celebrity persona to mobilize fair trade practices in ecological consciousness and ethically sustainable collections. Here, author Luis Fernando Romo examines how glamour and fashion become increasingly intertwined through ritualized fashion catwalks and forge a rhetoric of glamour that is rich and luxurious. Bibi Russell, who once collaborated with luxury brands and high-end magazines, reverses associated capitalist logic into making an under-recognized nexus of (ethical) beauty and poverty visible. She uses the celebrity capital of her name to promote local artisans in the garment industry and shift attention from exploitation in glamour to ethical production and consumption of glamour.

In mapping future directions of ethical models, Birte Fritsch and Patrick Nogly point out the significance of using the theoretical lens of eco-feminism and critically engaging literary texts in which fashion is written and read. In their chapter, "Echoes Of Ecofeminism: The Resonance of Glamour Labor and (Somatic) Ethics in Contemporary Literature," the offer close readings of Frédéric Beigbeders novel Au secours pardon (2007) to reflect on the socio-political discourse on fashion, fashion industry and physical glamour labor (Wissinger) in contemporary literary production. The authors highlight the nexus of high culture and haute couture and their intertwined discursive potentials instead of consuming literary productions that reinforce biopolitics in beauty. In doing so, they point out the specific role women need to take in and outside the fashion sphere to resist domination and exploitation of nature in the Anthropocene.

In the final chapter, "From Journalism to Fashion Activism: Refashioning Stories for Social Change," Samita Nandy shares an interview with Kabir Bedi and demonstrates how fashion activism is one of the key ways to address issues in glamour labor. Journalistic data and academic texts have shown that aesthetic expressions and visual storytelling around fashion are playing a key role in the publicity and promotion of many public figures' ethical brands and their activism. This brings us to an essential question: can students and fans refashion stories and normalize some of the much-needed democratic practices in celebrity activism, journalism, and academic studies involving popular culture? If not, what are the ethical issues at play in tabloid journalism that must be addressed in journalism schools and larger social institutions? The interview will explore the answers to these questions. In the interview, Kabir Bedi draws on his celebrity activism experience in Hollywood and Bollywood, and points out sustainable fashion as one of the key forms of aesthetic communication to resolve the dichotomy of the tabloid press in glamour.

While the book leaves readers with future directions, the Centre for Media and Celebrity Studies (CMCS) continues to take the question of free, accessible, unbiased communication and network building seriously and to implement further actions to challenge bias in celebrity journalism and fan culture. Over the past seven years, CMCS has brought together famous academics, public intellectuals, cultural critics, and celebrity activists in a particular effort to bridge the gaps between higher education and media. By dint of myriad projects, including conferences, seminars, and webinars, CMCS has emerged as a leader in the integration of research and media skills training with public discourses of fame. Although individual research projects and activities are crucial in the advancement of the field of celebrity studies, the need for a visible and inclusive platform, which serves to unify diverse people and ideas, cannot be understated. CMCS is novel in its approach to transforming the concepts of materiality and space as a response to this necessity. On the one hand, CMCS understands the importance of having individuals interact face-to-face and it promotes opportunities for the sharing of ideas and academic collaboration in progressive ways such as non-linear seating arrangements, interdisciplinary gap-bridging activities founded in practice-based research projects, the inclusion of performative practices, and eco-friendly vegan food in open spaces, all of which have been consistent in maintaining discourses of anti-oppression and incredibly fruitful in redefining networking as creating connections with value. Not only does CMCS implement the theories and approaches it espouses, it is ever forward-looking and is currently planning a studio and gallery setting where scholars can act as self-reflective practitioners and further media relations as citizen journalists. On the other hand, CMCS recognizes the power of a free and unhindered exchange of thought and research. Differences in nationality, social status, education, and experience should not prohibit individuals from having genuine and meaningful discussions. As a result of its online endeavors, CMCS is able to connect, and connect with, academic and non-academic individuals throughout the world, ultimately enriching fashion and celebrity studies.

We hope that the variety and scope of the chapters in the following book project highlight the unifying power of the Centre for Media and Celebrity Studies. Authors of this book have been incredibly dynamic in their ability to create both physical and virtual spaces where academics, activists, influencers, and media scholars alike can bridge the gaps between peoples, places, academia, and the media industry. Our sincere thanks to Cardiff University faculty Elliot Pill and RMIT University faculty Hilary Wheaton for their editorial contributions to this piece of work. We trust that the sources below and the following foreword will further bring promise to all readers in generating exciting and urgent changes in the fashion world of glamour.

References

Avis, M., Forbes, S., & Ferguson, S. (2014). The brand personality of rocks: A critical evaluation of a brand personality scale. *Marketing Theory*, 14(4), 451–475.

Bourdieu, P. (1984). *Distinction: A Social Critique of the Judgment of Taste*. (R. Nice, Trans). Cambridge: Harvard University Press.

Davies, G and Rose Chun. (2003). The Use of Metaphor in the Exploration of the Brand Concept. *Journal of Marketing Management,* (19) 45-71.

Entwistle, J., & Rocamora, A. (2006). The field of fashion materialized: A study of London Fashion Week. *Sociology*, 40 (4), 735-51.

Gander, M. (2014). Managing your personal brand. *Perspectives: Policy and Practice in Higher Education*.18 (3), 99-102.

Goffman, Erving (1959). *The Presentation of Self in Everyday Life*. Garden City, N.Y.: Doubleday.

Marshall, D., Christopher Moore and Kim Barbour (2015). Persona as method: exploring celebrity and the public self through persona studies. *Celebrity Studies*, 6 (3).

Nandy, S. (2015). *Scholars as Critics* media workshop. Presented at Bridging Gaps: Where is the Persona in Celebrity and Journalism?, New York City.

Halliday, R. (2016). "Front Row Aspirations in the Online Era: Bodies, Accessories and Fashioning Celebrity". In Jackie Raphael, Basuli Deb, and Nidhi Shrivasta (Eds). *Building Bridges in Celebrity Studies*. Toronto: WaterHill Publishing.

Tietje, Louis and Steven Cresap (2005). "Is Lookism Unjust?: The Ethics of Aesthetics and Public Policy Implications." *Journal of Libertarian Studies*, 19 (2), 31-50.

Wheaton, H. and Samita Nandy (2019). "Celebrity Activists: The Value-forms of Persona, Scandal, and Commodities." In Nathan Farrell (ed.). *The Political Economy of Celebrity Activism*. London: Routledge.

PART I:
Fashion in Famous Brands - 'Glamour Labour' in Fame

No More Than a Brand: Debating Lilti on Glory Essentialism

Adrian Wesołowski

Abstract. Apart from individual case studies, celebrity research, in its recently growing popularity, provided us with a solid foundation of the social functioning of fame. This resulted in a plethora of new analytical terms, such as honor, reputation, prestige, renown, social recognition, and celebrity itself being used to delineate various molds or understandings of being famous. This short research note explains why there have been few attempts at defining glory as a similar category and proposes, somehow subversively, that glory does not meet sufficient requirements to be considered a distinct form of fame. However, what is popularly understood as glory could be researched as two other themes – commemoration and aspiration.

Keywords: fame, celebrity, glory, methodology.

Introduction

One of the best-versed of celebrity scholars, Graeme Turner, finished his complex, modular definition of celebrity with a humble acknowledgment that the social function of celebrity could be understood better (Turner 2014, p. 10). To some, this was as much a fair judgment as a proof of the impotence of yet another new branch of cultural studies. In part, celebrity studies themselves are guilty of ossifying their image as research into mere 'pseudo-events'. The major area of interest for scholars working within the young tradition is the modern fame industry excrescent to marketing strategies that tend to be disregarded as irrelevant by the more orthodox academicians. The shallow world of media hypes and gossip culture extends its stigma to academia: celebrity is a nuisance, and therefore celebrity research has to be equally vapid.

Following this logic, only those figures that actually deserve fame would make an object worth studying, as biographical and hagiographical traditions suggest. This distinction mirrors the contrast between the deserved and undeserved fame, a popular conviction long recognized by celebrity scholars (Braudy 1986, pp. 6-8; Marshall, 1997, pp. ix-xiii). What follows is a form of essentialism. Celebrity scholars and their critics alike often see celebrities as ephemeral, discourse-dependent, and hedonism-oriented, categorically different from the public figures worthy of respect – real heroes, philanthropists, saints, etc. This difference translates to methods: celebrities are approached with the entire poststructuralist artillery, but those deserving fame meet with what Chris Rojek called the subjectivist approach (Rojek 2001, pp. 29-33).

This volume strives to prove a different point. Celebrity, as made evident by subsequent chapters, appeals to audiences not only because of aesthetics, but also because of ethics. The supposedly shallow fame can be used to support charitable actions; modern saints reap all the benefits of the market celebrity mechanisms; fans model their lifestyle as well as their morals after their idols. This calls fame essentialism into question. Is there actually a kind of fame that stands out from celebrity because of its self-contained moral worth? This text's aim is to diffuse the illusion that celebrities substituted the older, nobler species of famous people and to demystify ethical glamour, presenting it as a mechanism of fame rather than its substance. For this reason, I consider the feasibility of the only existing essentialist definition of glory and offer alternative solutions to approaching people usually regarded as famous in this way.

In Search of a Theory: Lilti and Glory

The belief that fame was once based on true achievement and moral worth is not new. Braudy noted that in our view of the past, "the process of fame seemed much simpler and the special nature of the famous much easier to appreciate (...) [T]he terms of the competition were clearer, and the contenders ideal figures, not the locusts of today" (Braudy 1986, pp. 8-10). While for a social scientist it could seem obvious that "such Golden Ages of true worth and justified fame never existed", most people are not so easily persuaded that the distinction in question is but a matter of convention. In result, we almost never treat it as a serious subject of analysis or scrutiny. As difficult as it is to even find a name for this mythical deserved kind of fame, both the common language and the professional literature seem to refer to the same group of connotations while discussing *glory* (although one could find other names – see Segal 1983; Dickson 2012; Kuehner 2016). This being said, there is almost no example of a theoretical dissection of glory, let alone in comparison to celebrity. In that regard, an outstanding attempt was made by Antoine Lilti in his *Invention of Celebrity* (2017).

Lilti traced the emergence of modern celebrity back to a period between 1750 and 1850. This timeframe, perhaps counter-intuitively, can contribute a lot to our understanding of glory. The eighteenth century was a time of drastic changes in the history of fame. Fame became more egalitarian, more market-dependent, and referred to personality rather than heroic achievement. (Braudy 1986, pp. 315-380; Rojek 2001, pp. 120-124; Morgan 2011, pp. 101-108). The old notion of hero was then challenged by the marketed popularity of actors, singers, and dancers. As Lilti argued, this was the time when some of the key constituents of modern celebrity were created, and the concept was slowly becoming distinct as an ephemeral, superficial, and easily monetized popularity based on collective curiosity in the intimate lives of the famous. By contrasting it with emerging celebrity, Lilti (2017) was able to pinpoint the most characteristic, defining features of glory:

> Glory designates notoriety acquired by someone who is judged to be extraordinary because of his or her achievements, whether these are acts of bravery, or artistic or literary works. It is essentially a posthumous designation and flourishes through the commemoration of the hero in the collective memory (...) glory concerns heroes, saints, illustrious men – all the figures whose glorification has played a major role in Western culture (...) glory can only come from the serene judgment of posterity embodied by 'cultural institutions and people of good taste' (pp. 4-7)

Lilti's pioneering attempt to operationalize glory deserves careful attention. If fame essentialism was correct, the Enlightenment would constitute a period when glory lost its dominance to celebrity. The advantages of the historical period Lilti analyzed and innovative nature of his undertaking makes his definition a good starting point of theoretical reflection about glory.

Defining Glory

For the needs of analysis, Lilti's definition can be broken down into the following points:

> 1: Glory has to do with strongly positive feelings, admiration and distinguishment.

> 2: Glory is based on meritocratic measures, awarded to 'extraordinary people' in reaction to their achievements.

> 3: Glory lasts long. In opposition to celebrity, which flourishes and wilts quickly, it is 'universal and ageless'.

> 4: Glory is awarded mostly posthumously by posterity.

This definition seems to encapsulate both the thoughts of Lilti and the common convictions that exist until today. However, it is far from being perfect. Throughout Lilti's book, the line between his analytic terms and the historical ideas he discussed blurs. Moreover, the figures presented in the book often use words such as celebrity and glory interchangeably, in both of the distinguished meanings (Lilti 2017, pp. 86-101). Without depriving the book's basic claims of their validity, this ambiguity limits the use of the definition strictly to the context of France in the eighteenth century. Furthermore, Lilti's approach is, in essence, that of history of ideas. This is problematic as social phenomena such as celebrity and glory cannot be truthfully explained in a definition limited to the sphere of public perception or collective imagination. What must be taken into account are processes exterior to that sphere and embedded in social practices, such as methods of disseminating news about a celebrity, together with their impact. In order to properly distinguish between different molds of fame, one needs to recognize alternative social structures standing behind them.

This is something that the above definition fails to achieve. Lilti defines glory and reputation for the purpose of creating analytic indicators of where celebrity does not reach – or, in simpler terms, to delineate the definition of celebrity (Lilti 2017, pp. 3-4). For that need, celebrity is often juxtaposed with glory as being short-lived and provoking curiosity as opposed to the long-lasting and deserved admiration. Meanwhile, the more inclusive historical approaches to celebrity see it not through the association with curiosity and ephemerality but emphasize the increasing reach and impact of media or the existence of celebrity cultures instead (Morgan 2011). In these accounts, celebrity expands its meaning to include the popular notions of glory, as generals, religious figures and writers are subjected to the same mechanisms of recognition as actors and socialites. In other words, the contents of fame (meanings ascribed to a celebrated figure) are of secondary significance to the forms of fame (mechanisms of dissemination as well as the quantity and quality of public opinion). Therefore, Lilti's take on celebrity and glory does not merely neglect the social dimension of fame; it stands only as long as we accept the reductive view of celebrity itself.

There are reasons to think that the four points being the basis of Lilti's definition are not only insufficient for a proper description of glory, but on their own are useless in differentiating between glory and celebrity understood as independent social phenomena. This is certainly true in case of points one and two: the strongly positive reception does not have to but might be a feature of celebrity as well, and the meritocratic condition – one's glory based on their extraordinary deeds – is virtually a repetition of what Rojek described as achieved celebrity (2001, pp. 17-20). Point four entails a burden of defining yet another term, posterity. It is not clear who among the successors has the honor of awarding glorious status and how it occurs. The claim of posterity being embodied by "cultural institutions and people of good taste", as one of Lilti's figures would have it, is just as vague. Again formed in opposition to celebrity, it obviously exempts common people – the "multitude of idiots" (Lilti 2017, p. 23) – from having a say in establishing who is glorious and gives no grounds for such an exclusion. Left alone, point three, however valid, does not seem to provide a meaningful distinction. The claims of universality and eternity of glory are empirically empty. Revisiting some of the earliest examples of individuals regarded glorious, Homer or Alexander the Great, a period taken into account amounts to mere few thousand years. Can we meaningfully assume that their memory is eternal? Even remembering that Lilti could derive his wording from the sources, can we believe in the universality of a common agreement on who should be considered glorious while the status is awarded by a loosely defined 'posterity'? If all that is the case, is it feasible to argue that glory is just one form of celebrity characterized by glamour (as opposed to notoriety) and being remembered longer?

For a celebrity studies scholar, such a definition of glory does not only blur into celebrity; it loses its utility. Our understanding of the glorious has to be limited to the aforementioned contents of fame; in researching it, we are bound to trace the history of one concept rather than a set of social practices. Apart from Lilti's, the attempts to define glory are almost non-existent; when they appear, the definitions are rather suggested than directly presented. In order to properly describe glory, we would need to clearly determine social practices standing behind it, including the media involved in the glorification; to clarify if a person has to be dead in order to be glorified, and if not, in what circumstances can they be alive; whether they can be fictional; how "universal" must the admiration be to be called glory, which groups have to be engaged in this admiration and how many people does it take; finally, what is the history of glory. As long as glory remains undefined, the essentialist position fails. If there are no identified social practices and meanings that could help us delineate such a definition, it is reasonable to assume glory does not exist as a distinct kind of fame.

However, I would claim that our common intuitions are not entirely wrong in associating certain social phenomena with glory, even though it remains undefined. Two elements that are usually related to glory are indeed related to each other, and it is worthwhile to further our understanding of them. These are commemoration (collective monumentalization) and aspiration (an end-line in the horizon of fame).

Demystifying Glory: The Aftermath

The instinctive aspect of the long-lasting glory (the immortalization, the ultimate goal of fame) is problematically irreducible. No definition of celebrity would be so wide as to encompass a condition of ceremonial remembrance, while such a ritual is not in any way surprising in the case of individuals attributed with glory. This encapsulates the posthumous recognition and explains the claims for the 'eternal' immortality of a glorified figure that 'lives on' by being collectively memorized or symbolized; it involves both social practices generating material remains (monuments, commemorative plaques, institutions under-the-name-of) and the place of heroes in the contemporary discourse; it is directly related to monumentalization, the collective aggrandizement of historical figures which, mostly dead, are credited with the historical agency. And yet, we cannot simply equate glory with commemoration, mostly because the latter comes with its own set of problems. For example, it would be misleading to ascribe an inherently positive coloring of glory to commemoration – that would result in glorifying, say, Adolf Hitler, who is remembered in today's public sphere as an overwhelmingly dark figure (Williams 2017). Hitler has his own *lieux de mémoire*, whether we consider as such the Nazi-centered museum in Munich or just any WWII memorial inevitably linked with his name (with Auschwitz-Birkenau concentration camp at the fore). More than that, he is still the pop world's universal adversary or, according to Mike Godwin's famous remark in his "Meme, counter-meme" article, a basis of bitter accusation of foul play if one uses his example in any sort of discussion (as I just did). In other words, Hitler is memorized, symbolized, and monumentalized, clearly an object of unintended commemoration, but by no means glorified. Not only good men are commemorated.

Interestingly, such approach would draw the theme of glory away from research on forms of fame and towards memory studies, cultural heritage studies, and memetics. In the latter area, glory already gained some scholarly interest for attempting to answer the question of how the desire of immortalization fits in the overarching scheme of creative mimesis, a specific take on cultural reproduction. In a chapter of a book he edited, Thomas Ryba (2014) argued that the desire for being remembered and emulated, the eternalization of one's meme set is analogous to the need of perpetuating one's bloodline (gene set). His reflection, strongly based on historical study of the semantic horizon of glory in Western thought, serves as a good example of the usefulness of memetics, a much-needed link between biological and social sciences, which has not acquired sufficiently serious treatment since the publication of *The Selfish Gene* by Richard Dawkins (1976).

What is still missing from the above-mentioned criteria of glory is an aspect that has less to do with sociology and much more with social psychology: aspiration. Popular culture as well as multiple celebrity studies use the term 'glory' to designate an idea of worthy fame, flattering recognition that one is able to acquire when they achieve enough to deserve it, no matter that neither its accurate definition nor mechanisms of its functioning are presented (e.g., see an otherwise fascinating text by Chanu 2010). There is an instinctive sense of what glory is – or ought to be – but it is presented in terms of superlatives, not observable phenomena. Oftentimes contrasted with celebrity, these formulations serve as a horizontal end line of what it is capable of offering. In other words, glory is most often presented as the aim of fame rather than a kind of it, as something to strive for rather than something to handle, as transcendent rather than existing. In this sense, glory is alluded to as much today as ever before, including the work of Lilti. However, as aspiration lies at the center of so-understood glory, its study should focus on individual psychology and intellectual exchange instead of claiming the ground of celebrity studies.

In other words, while current research suggests that there is nothing essential about fame of the people we consider glorious, one can imagine studying ways of commemorating historical figures and development of individual attitudes towards achieving glorious recognition. The set of intuitive connotations related to glory should not trickle down to our research. Instead, the fame of figures such as Mother Teresa, Abraham Lincoln, or Martin Luther could be comprehensively presented respectively (1) as celebrity or renown while they were alive, (2) as their individual inclination towards being famous, and (3) as their posthumous monumentalization, all social and psychological phenomena that are well-known to us.

This leaves us with a bit depressing, but not unexpected conclusion: we cannot recognize any figures as universally praiseworthy, but we are able to observe that there are people we glorify individually or collectively because of subjective or (at best) intersubjective reasons. Glory is no more than a brand. What does it mean for the study of celebrity today? Does it necessarily translate to glory being only a mask, another type of public persona created for the needs of an audience responsive to the ethical appeal? Will market relations prevail as a way of understanding why we collectively look up to certain people? In what measure is the capitalist economy a moral one? While all of these questions are yet to be answered, a distinct notion of figures that deserve fame according to some universal standard becomes less and less convincing; the matter in more than one way becomes the song of the past.

References

Braudy, L. (1986). *The Frenzy of Renown. Fame and its History*. Oxford: Oxford University Press.

Chanu, A. (2010). From Paths of Glory to Celebrity Boulevards: Sociology of Paris Match Covers, 1949-2005. *Revue française de sociologie, 51*(5), 69-116.

Dickson, G. (2012). Charisma, Medieval and Modern. *Religions, 3*(3), 763-789.

Dawkins, R. (1976). *The Selfish Gene*. New York: Oxford University Press.

Kuehner, C. (2016). Eternal Fame? Honour and Prestige in Historical Perspective. *helden. heroes. Héros*, *3*(2), 11-15.

Lilti, A. (2017). *The Invention of Celebrity, 1750-1850*. Cambridge: Polity Press.

Marshall, D. (1997). *Celebrity and Power: Fame in contemporary culture*. Minneapolis: University of Minnesota Press.

Morgan, S. (2011). Celebrity: academic 'pseudo-event' or a useful concept for historians? *Cultural and social history, 8*(1), 95-114.

Rojek, C. (2001). *Celebrity*. London: Reaktion Books.

Ryba, T. (2014). Mimesis and Immortal Glory: How Creativity is Spurred by the Desire for One's Ideas to Dominate the Meme Pool. In: V.N. Redekop, T. Ryba et al. (Eds.), *Rene Girard and Creative Mimesis* (123-142). Plymouth: Lexington Books.

Segal, C. (1983). Kleos and its Ironies in the Odyssey. *L'antiquité classique 52*, 22-47.

Turner, G. (2010). Approaching celebrity studies. *Celebrity Studies 1*(1), 11-20.

Turner, G. (2014). *Understanding celebrity*. London: Sage.

Williams, S. M. (2017). The celebrification of Adolf Hitler. *Celebrity Studies 8*(1), 1-5.

Towards an Ethnography of Mediated Celebrity Glamour

Lori Hall-Araujo

Abstract. This chapter describes media research methods and research-framing theories engaged for a study of social media use among a discrete group of college-age women in the United States. The chapter offers a framework for those engaging in similar qualitative research and includes the results of study participants' attitudes about intersecting themes of persona branding, appropriate social media use, and idealizing systems for beauty, fashion, and celebrity culture. Given the rapidly evolving and increasingly globalized communication genre of social media, the process here described can be useful to practitioners and scholars from a range of disciplines.

Keywords: social media, media ideologies, media research methods.

Introduction

The aim of this chapter is to provide a process—informed by an interdisciplinary background that includes anthropological training—for conducting research on how people use and understand media, particularly social media. The framework provides a series of steps: asking a research question; identifying the community or public to whom the question pertains; addressing potential ethical concerns; analyzing data collected from multiple sites; and sharing the results here. The chapter is designed to encourage an ongoing dialogue by bridging disciplinary and professional disjunctions.

The Process

Step 1: Asking the question

Social media for young people is often the primary conduit for learning about current events, celebrity culture, and banal and thrilling moments in the lives of their friends, family, and acquaintances. Moreover, social media is a space where themes of celebrity culture, beauty ideals, fashion, commodification, and branding intersect. What if the medium also facilitates the circulation of ethical imperatives?

In *Perfect Me* (Widdows, 2018), philosopher Heather Widdows posits that beauty is becoming a global ethical ideal as standards are getting homogenized for thinness, firmness, smoothness, and youth. This ideal is reaching global proportions thanks to social media's reach and an increasingly visual culture. Since at least Plato, there has been a longstanding association between external beauty and virtue. One finds a contemporary example in animated children's films, which teach and reinforce that goodness is beautiful and evil is ugly. What has changed in the 21st century is the sheer reach and rapid circulation of beauty ideals that can put the spotlight on any ordinary individual with social media access.

Though people have always engaged in grooming and beautifying practices, Widdows suggests what is new and what she condemns, are global internalized systems of self-policing as described by Michel Foucault in *Discipline and Punish: The Birth of the Prison* (Foucault, 1975), whereby prisoners in a Panopticon know the guard is in the center yet never know when they are being surveilled (see figure 1). Consequently, they behave at all times as if being monitored. For Widdows, social media and the selfie lead to a kind of beauty and fashion Panopticon experience for participants. I sought to put this notion to the test in a study of young women's engagement with social media.

Fig. 1. A Panopticon in practice. Prison guard in a security tower, Stateville Penitentiary, Joliet, Illinois, USA. Underwood Photo Archives.

Step 2: Identifying the community

Recent new media research finds that users encounter an at times unwanted blurring of their different social spheres. This can be attributed to a 21st century cultural shift whereby the individual is understood to be a business to be managed and branded. Competent brand management means presenting one's "authentic self" for which there can be no variation depending upon social context (Gershon, 2017, pp. 24-27).

The practice of self-branding might have begun with people whose bodies are their 'business'—such as fashion models—yet self-branding is an increasingly common phenomenon in a gig economy (Gershon, 2017). According to Elizabeth Wissinger's 2015 study of fashion models, models are told, "You must be the CEO of you, it's your own responsibility for your success . . ." (p.5). As CEO of you-the-brand, practitioners maintain their brand image through social media posts, blogging, and so on in what Wissinger calls "glamour labor" (pp.6-7).

Women's colleges are typically dedicated to women's empowerment, so I wondered to what extent fashion program students at the institution where I teach would resist homogenizing beauty imperatives. The college's students are encouraged to be reflexive about their social media practices, so I expected they would give considerable thought to circulating beauty standards and their own beauty labor.

Step 3: Ethics concerns

When U.S. students and faculty engage in human subjects research—whether clinical or qualitative—accredited colleges and universities require them to submit a research description to an institutional review board for approval. With fewer than 700 full-time residential undergraduates and about 40 full-time faculty, the college is smaller than some high schools. For my research to be effective, students needed to feel safe speaking to me freely without fear of repercussions from me or anyone else, including their peers.

While there were students who expressed no concern about maintaining their anonymity and even offered to pose for a photograph so readers could see who they were, I had an ethical responsibility to anonymize all students' identities. Therefore I have omitted some details to preserve individuals' privacy.

Step 4: Collecting data

I collected data by examining circulating media including magazines, newspapers and news sites, and public social media accounts, and conducting field research consisting of interviews with participants and observation.

Field research, whether observing behavior or conducting interviews, requires the researcher to have a degree of competency in the communicative modes and some understanding of the community's referential universe (Briggs, 1986, pp. 54-55). To supplement my competency, I enlisted the assistance of a graduating senior, a fashion communication major. The student shared her insider knowledge with me and offered interpretations of campus social dynamics.

I interviewed a total of seven students from different majors within the college's fashion program. The students ranged in age from nineteen- to twenty-six-years-old. Each recorded interview lasted about an hour and was conducted at an off-campus café.

Step 5: Interpreting the data

My approach is informed by performance studies (Bauman, 1984 [1977]), which asserts that an expressive communication event—such as a social media post—has meanings generated by the creator/speaker, which may be different from the meaning(s) ascribed by the audience or recipient(s). In my analysis I look for elements of individual agency among creators and recipients and disjuncture in meanings.

All participants had social media accounts at the time of the interviews while several had deleted and re-established accounts over the years. Instagram was overwhelmingly the preferred platform. Among those who connect via social media, some said they feel they get a truer sense of who a person is by looking at their Instagram feed. One participant told me that if someone's Instagram feed looks "uninspired," she might decide not to follow them even if they are friends in everyday life. Another said, "I'm not stingy with my follows," yet also acknowledged choosing not to follow someone if they only had a few things she liked on their feed. When I assessed participants' practices and reflections on how they interpret others' social media feeds, I noticed a pattern emerge: users interpret the mediated self as an expression of one's authentic self. Media can be a conduit for circulating some representation of a person, which is what I mean by mediated self. The circulating form, such as a social media post, is both a reservoir and reference point for information (Spitulnik, 1997). Among the people I spoke to, it was important that the mediated self be the authentic self. So, what is the authentic self?

In her 2017 publication, which assesses the impact of social media on job hunting, anthropologist Ilana Gershon finds job seekers are advised to express their authentic selves on social media. The idea is that the authentic self should be a person's 'brand,' an unchanging and coherent persona across contexts because it is 'real.' Branding oneself in this way supposedly benefits the jobseeker because it signals to potential employers the promise of a consistent, unchanging, employable version of themselves. In Gershon's study, most people wanted their branded self to align with their imagined authentic self.

Fig. 2. An Instagram post by the plus-size model, Barbie Ferreira. (2018, December 17) Retrieved from Instagram, @barbienox

The women I spoke to demonstrated a comparable understanding in their approach to presentation of self on social media. This was the case whether it was assessing someone else's or their own feed in the pursuit of authenticity. Although participants were savvy, recognizing the degree to which social media posts are often highly constructed, they nonetheless made distinctions between, as graduating senior, Ingrid put it, "beauty that masks you" and "beauty that reveals you." Ingrid, who admires the plus-size model Barbie Ferreira (Instagram handle @barbienox) added, "she is all about showing her natural self . . . and I think that is so cool." Nonetheless, perusing Ferreira's Instagram feed, one quickly discovers no unflattering images. Most posts appear to be selfies or photos taken of the model alone, possibly serving as a branded image calling card to help Ferreira secure modeling gigs. Though the model appears at times without makeup or nearly nude, what is arguably "natural" in the feed are those images showcasing the model's curvaceous figure, which is outside mainstream fashion ideals. Nonetheless, Barbie has smooth skin, normative gender-specific proportions, is young, and quite beautiful. Participants in my study tended to regard this kind of social media persona as authentic and admirable though it is nonetheless mediated through application filters and careful image creation and selection (see figure 2). Comments included expressions of envy, encouragement, and sexual interest.

The women I interviewed understand the beauty labor involved in trying to achieve such 'natural' beauty. They expressed that creating such an authentic self on social media can be burdensome. Six of the seven participants stated openly or otherwise implied they feel some degree of pressure to labor over their personal appearance if including images of themselves on social media. For one woman, the entire feed needs to be cohesive even when the photos are of inanimate objects. She told me about a time she removed a photo because it did not align with the overarching themes on her Instagram feed, which has been described as having "weird, cool shit." The photo she removed was of a garment she had made. While she said she did not like the way it looked alongside the other images on her feed, it struck me that posting photos of one's fashion designs puts one in a considerably more vulnerable position than posting images of weird, cool shit. Photos of oneself or one's creations subject a person—and by extension the branded persona—to greater external scrutiny.

Most of the participants described themselves as primarily passive consumers of social media content; that is, they do not frequently post but they do check out what others post on Instagram at least once a day. Nicole told me she used to be very active on Instagram until strangers began shouting out her handle to her in public, which prompted her to delete all social media accounts. She has since created new accounts but not without reservations. In everyday life Nicole did not feel obliged to dress up but for social media she needed to look her best, which was a costly endeavor. In preparation for graduation (and presumably lots of social media posts), she had spent $300 on human hair extensions plus another $200 to have it styled and $75 for a manicure. Because Nicole couldn't afford such beauty maintenance on a regular basis, she mostly preferred to use social media passively and seldom post.

At least five of the women expressed their preference for "natural," "authentic," or "unique" beauty and fashion images. When I asked them to show me examples of social media "influencers" whose images and mediated personas they liked, they invariably showed me examples of women who mostly hewed to some combination of at least three of the homogenized beauty qualities Heather Widdows describes: thinness, firmness, smoothness, and youth (e.g. see figure 2). At least two women told me they like models who are not model thin, yet provided examples of women who are otherwise firm, smooth, young, and conventionally attractive such as Sabina Karlsson and Barbie Ferreira.

A pattern emerged suggesting participants felt pressure to present themselves as "natural," "authentic," and "unique" while aligning in some way with beauty standards for thinness, firmness, smoothness, and youth. One woman told me she likes to see "real, raw images" of others because she feels it provides insight into the "real" person. Yet this attractive young woman told me she only posts "perfect" photos of herself that she achieves "naturally." The emphasis on naturalness and perfect authenticity among the participants led me to wonder if these factors were not particular to the culture of a women's college, where students are encouraged to be feminists. The majority of participants did not admit to liking mainstream beauty ideals even as their social media practices demonstrated considerable self-policing and platform management of their brand. A willingness to post only those images of themselves that met their criteria for naturalness and authenticity translated into participants refraining from posting very often, a kind of self-policing by omission. One woman told me that when she takes photos of friends, she always asks for permission before posting the image because she wants to make sure her friends are satisfied with how they are being represented; a quasi-copyright permission request.

Participants' media ideologies—that is, their "beliefs about how a medium communicates and structures communication" (Gershon, 2010)—varied considerably when it came to different social media platforms. For example, although all participants had Instagram accounts, their attitudes included the following: Instagram should be for personal use only; Instagram is for professional purposes only; one should have separate accounts for personal and professional purposes; and, in the case of two women, an account should be authentic and whole where the personal and professional are elided into a single "brand" image. Despite wide-ranging attitudes about Instagram, the women were unanimous in their cautious approach to social media use. Most told me they post images of themselves infrequently because doing so requires so much work.

The campus culture's implicitly understood interpersonal norms seemed to hold a powerful sway in terms of influencing social media practices. For example, all of the participants agreed that overtly political statements were to be avoided. When one of the participants, Alex, made a political gesture on her public Instagram account, she experienced considerable backlash.

Alex was unusual among those I interviewed for a couple of reasons. First, she was the only person who told me she liked having incoherent and even embarrassing images of herself on different social media platforms, which she found amusing. Alex was also unique in her willingness to post an image with a political message, a position that eventually created problems for her prompting a reconsideration of how she uses social media.

Earlier that spring Alex attended a fraternity party where someone took a photo of her dressed in party attire, smiling in front of a U.S. flag. She posted the photo and included the caption, "Make America Great Again" (see figure 3 for an example of this social media political image genre, albeit not Alex's actual photo).

Fig. 3. An Instagram post by @_annapaulina representing a post 2016-presidential election trend. Sheets, M. (2017, August 26) Poolside politics, Daily Mail. Retrieved from https://www.dailymail.co.uk

Within 24 hours of Alex's public Instagram post, college peers wrote negative comments on her account and several students confronted her in person. Though Alex denied ill will and admitted no wrongdoing, she removed the photo to avoid escalating the issue. Alex was the only person I spoke to who expressed feeling social pressure to remove an Instagram post. According to Alex, who was raised near a military base, the photo and caption were meant to be patriotic.

The fallout Alex experienced aligned with what participants repeated in their interviews. Not only are they reluctant to post imperfect images, every single woman—including Alex—told me she is reluctant to engage in any kind of political discourse online, regardless of her political persuasion.

Since the 2016 presidential election, a social media trend has emerged whereby politically conservative, attractive young women post photos of themselves in front of U.S. flags (e.g. see figure 3). At the other end of this trend spectrum are images of women with guns, flags, and "Make America Great Again" (MAGA) paraphernalia (e.g. see figure 4). Presumably Alex and her critics were attuned to this trend. Alex told me that after the incident, she decided to make her Instagram account private again.

Fig. 4. An Instagram post by @babesfortrump representing a post 2016-presidential election trend. Sheets, M. (2017, August 26) Poolside politics, Daily Mail. Retrieved from https://www.dailymail.co.uk

Conclusion

There is sometimes the sense that images "don't lie," a dangerous presumption in an era of widely circulating images. Images are created and received within particular contexts and often they are accompanied by words, further contextualizing their meaning. In the early 21st century, such circulating mediated images might be framed as "texts" in the sociolinguistic sense insofar as they can be detached from one context and get repeated, quoted or re-posted, and commented upon (Barber, 2007, p.3). Social media expedites the ease and speed with which an image or post is detached and recontextualized via its transmission and reception.

The young women I spoke to understood the power of circulating images on social media, hence their reluctance to post actively and publicly whether the post has a selfie or a political perspective. Yet, such self-policing does not entirely prevent one from becoming somebody else's mediated text image. While none of the women I spoke to is entirely absent from social media, they post infrequently and participate passively. Posting images of themselves—which seems to be an unspoken expectation for participating on social media and means for expressing one's agency—requires intense beauty labor in order to meet shared general understandings for what constitutes desired naturalness and authenticity. When students follow mainstream celebrity figures who showcase a labor-intensive appearance, such as Kim Kardashian or Mariah Carey, they seem chiefly to enjoy the spectacle of the figure. The other celebrities, models, and influencers whom they admire and follow are people they say meet their criteria for naturalness and authenticity. While this position seems on its surface to support feminist ideals, the reality is that the women my participants characterize as "unique" and outside of mainstream beauty norms—models such as Adwoa Aboah, Barbie Ferreira, Sabina Karlsson, and Celina Leroy—nonetheless conform to at least three of the homogenizing criteria Heather Widdows says are becoming global standards for beauty as an ethical ideal: youth, thinness, firmness, and smoothness. By not recognizing the inflexibility of shared understandings about what constitutes acceptable uniqueness or authenticity, these young women risk supplanting previous rigid beauty ideals with new rigid beauty ideals. Moreover, what is especially distressing is that 21st century beauty ideals seem to have a moral imperative. It is no longer enough to appear beautiful; one must now labor to seem authentic and naturally, uniquely beautiful as an expression of feminist agency. Anything else "masks you."

Acknowledgments

I am grateful to the Stephens College community for supporting this project, especially: the Professional Development Committee and the Office of the Vice President of Academic Affairs for providing financial support to present at the 2018 *Bridging Gaps: Where is Ethical Glamour in Celebrity Culture?* conference in Lisbon; the students in my spring 2018 fashion history course for dynamic conversations about fashion, beauty ideals, and social media; the seven anonymous students who participated in the study and eagerly shared their insights; and Katherine Craig, who served as my research assistant and social media guru. I also wish to extend a heartfelt thanks to the two anonymous reviewers for their invaluable feedback on an earlier version of this chapter.

References

Barber, K. (2007). *The anthropology of texts, persons and publics: oral and written culture in Africa and beyond.* Cambridge: Cambridge University Press.

Bauman, R. (1984 [1977]). *Verbal art as performance.* Long Grove, IL: Waveland Press, Inc.

Briggs, C. L. (1986). *Learning how to ask: a sociolinguistic appraisal of the role of the interview in social science research.* Cambridge: Cambridge University Press.

Foucault, M. (1977). *Discipline and punish: the birth of the prison.* (A. Sheridan, Trans.) New York: Panteon Books. (Original work published 1975).

Gershon, I. (2010). *The breakup 2.0: disconnecting over new media.* New York: Cornell University Press.

Gershon, I. (2017a). *Down and out in the new economy: how people find (or don't find) work today.* Chicago: The University of Chicago Press.

Spitulnik, D. (1997). The Social Circulation of Media Discourse and the Mediation of Communities. *Journal of Linguistic Anthropology.* Vol. 6, no. 2: 161.187.

Widdows, H. (2018). *Perfect me: beauty as an ethical ideal.* Princeton: University Press.

Wissinger, E. A. (2015). *This year's model: fashion, media, and the making of glamour.* New York: New York University Press.

Non-Heteronormative Gender Performativity and the Discursive Value of Celebrity Brand Gesture: a Case Study

Olga Andreevskikh

Abstract. This chapter focuses on three brand gestures of Alexandre Vassiliev, Russian celebrity and host of the makeover TV show '*Fashion Verdict*' (*Modnyi Prigovor*). The analysis demonstrates how the celebrity brand gestures are used to mediate non-heteronormative sexuality and gender performance, at the same time contributing to the state-imposed discourse of 'traditional' sexuality.

Keywords: brand gesture, celebrity, non-heteronormative sexuality, gender performance.

The mediation of gender and sexual identities is an essential part of the overall discourse on sexuality and gender in contemporary Russia media (Strukov 2014). This chapter presents selected findings of a wider research project on LGBTQ discourses and construction of LGBTQ identities in contemporary Russian media[1]. It seeks to demonstrate how non-heteronormative transgressive brand gestures performed by a media celebrity serve to promote 'traditional values' as part of the state-sustained discourse of heteronormativity in the context of 'traditional sexuality' legislation.

Russian Federal Law 195 Article 6.21 of July 2013 against 'propaganda of non-traditional sexual relationships among minors' has made a considerable impact on Russian media in terms of portraying non-heteronormative sexual and gender identities. On the one hand, this law attempts to restrain freedom of speech in Russian media further and has therefore met diverse media responses resulting in a wide and complex range of LGBTQ media portrayals. On the other hand, it aims to introduce a restrictive binary societal approach to sexuality as 'traditional' vs 'non-traditional', which has mobilized and affected the evolving LGBTQ identities. These new identities, in their turn, while being the object of media construction, have been both challenging and shaping the

---

[1] The PhD research under the title 'Constructing LGBTQ identities: Russian media in the context of the 'traditional sexuality' legislation' has been conducted at the University of Leeds, UK, between 2015 and 2019.

current LGBTQ media discourse (Kondakov 2014, Persson 2014, Sperling 2015). In this context, any examples of mediation of non-heteronormative sexualities in mainstream Russian media cannot but evoke considerable research interest.

The lifestyle entertainment program '*Modnyi Prigovor*' (Fashion Verdict) has been broadcast on Russia's primary TV channel, *Pervyi Kanal* (Channel One), since 2007. The program imitates a court trial with Aleksandre Vassiliev, fashion historian, acting as the 'fashion judge'; Evelina Khromchenko, fashion expert and journalist, as the 'prosecutor'; and Nadezhda Babkina, a folk-pop star, as 'counsel for defense'. The plaintiff accuses the defendant, most invariably a woman, of violating the rules of fashion, and the trial results in the defendant's total makeover. Each episode evolves around the defendant being helped to balance a professional career and a successful personal life as mother and wife/partner, i.e., being urged to comply with the gender stereotype of 'double burden' common in contemporary Russian society, where 'double burden' stands for women combining the roles of a full-time housewife and a full-time worker (Stella 2014). Regardless of being broadcast in primetime on the most important state-owned TV channel and despite promoting so-called 'traditional Russian values' and stereotypical gendered behavior, this popular TV program mediates images which do not fit in the heteronormative gender and sexuality norms imposed by the official public discourse on 'traditional vs non-traditional' sexuality. The current research dwells upon one of such images – that of the fashion judge Alexandre Vassiliev.

Although the popular TV presenter has never made a public coming-out[2], Alexandre Vassiliev's flamboyant outfits, camp mannerisms, and intonations do not leave much room for doubts about his non-heteronormative sexuality. On the makeover show, he represents a stereotypical image of the 'artistic homosexual' (Baer 2009), an image which is traditionally viewed as positive in Russian culture: an artistic gay male is bound to help a woman look beautiful and to instruct her on how to attract male attention – an ability quite fitting to the purpose of the show. Vassiliev's extralinguistic behavior clearly characterizes him as a person of a non-stereotypical type of masculinity: his facial expressions are varied, diverse, vivid, and somewhat feminine; he never misses a chance to do a little flirtatious dance when there is a live music performance during the show. Vassiliev's idiosyncrasies result in him being perceived as an artistic aesthete, a connoisseur of fine arts and fashion, not necessarily recognized as a man of a 'non-traditional' sexuality, but definitely

---

[2] In general, coming-outs are an alien concept among contemporary Russian celebrities due to the overall homophobic societal trends.

viewed as different from a stereotypical Russian male and thus representing a 'non-traditional' masculinity.   Vassiliev's professional achievements, his recognition and his high position in society, as well as his connections with Russia and the West[3], put him above the 'anti-gay propaganda' law and enable him to venture types of behavior which could easily be interpreted as 'propaganda of non-traditional sexual relationships'.

It is important to note that the employment of openly (and stereotypically) gay male TV presenters as makeover show hosts is not a unique feature of the '*Fashion Verdict*' but rather a global media trend, which should not be confused with human rights and activist discourses of gay visibility (Kadir and Tidy 2013, Kolehmainen and Mäkinen 2011, Lovelock 2018). In programs such as '*How to Look Good Naked*' or '*Queer Eye for the Straight Guy*', gay presenters implement makeovers and transformations for heteronormative program participants, and it is the othering of the homosexual host that makes their queer gaze legitimate and acceptable: "although the usage of gay characters destabilizes prevailing conceptions of gender and sexuality, it can also participate in fortifying normative understandings of sexuality and gender. Also, in the context of reality television shows, (sub)cultural capital associated with only certain kinds of gay characters advances gay visibility in television" (Kolehmainen and Mäkinen 2011: 225). On the '*Fashion Verdict*' show, the stereotypical camp non-heteronormative sexuality performance of Alexandre Vassiliev helps him celebrate the traditional Russian femininity: he knows best how to make a woman look stylish and sexy, but his own gaze is not of sexual nature at all, and Vassiliev is, therefore, free to demonstrate transgressive verbal and non-verbal behavior, e.g., to use transgressive non-heteronormative gestures.

Specific brand gestures used by media personae consistently attract the attention of scholars interested in analyzing how the 'brand' gestures unique to a certain celebrity and common gestures used by various political and celebrity figures contribute to the public discourses they are involved in (see Hall et al. 2016, Navaretta 2016, Streeck 2008, Wehling 2009). In the contemporary celebrity and mediatized culture (Hall et al. 2016: 72), TV celebrities such as the Russian TV presenter and fashion historian Alexandre Vassiliev can also be viewed as powerful agents in public discourse.

It is difficult to overestimate the importance of gestures for the creation and perception of TV celebrities' brand identities. As rhetorician Hariman put it (1995), "To become a celebrity, one has to master and distinguish oneself

---

[3] Vassiliev has dual citizenship of France and the Russian Federation, and as a professional he is involved in a range of projects in Russia and in Europe.

within a rhetoric of gestures – virtually every star has a defining gesture or gestural effect" (cited in Hall et al. 2016: 81). Alexandre Vassiliev's mediated performance demonstrates a wide range of such gestures and gestural effects.

In the current paper, gestures are understood as:

> a label for actions that have the features of manifest deliberate expressiveness. They are those actions or those aspects of another's actions that, having these features, tend to be directly perceived as being under the guidance of the observed person's voluntary control and being done for the purposes of expression rather than in the service of some practical aim. (Kendon 2004:15)

The interpretation of Vassiliev's gestures comprises both their function in the linear speech discourse of the TV show narrative and their role in constructing an image of non-heteronormative gender and sexuality and in promoting the discourse of heternormativity. The presenter's bodily and head movements are analyzed as linked to the language he uses and to the overall discursive structure of the show. To reach the objective of the current research, three episodes of the program were selected and the brand gestures employed by Vassiliev in all of the selected episodes were analyzed.

The overall mission of the makeover program '*Fashion Verdict*' is linked to reinforcing traditional gender norms and promoting the 'correct' type of femininity – the one that would lead the woman to success in her personal life. In view of this, the episodes broadcast just before 8th March, International Women's Day, were chosen for the current analysis. International Women's Day has been celebrated globally since the early 1900s and is aimed at highlighting the social, economic, cultural, and political achievements of women. Initially, in post-revolutionary Russia, IWD was about the struggle for women's equality; however, throughout Soviet times and especially after the masculinity and femininity crises of the post-Soviet era, this holiday has evolved into a celebration of traditional stereotypical femininity, a day when women are given flowers and chocolates, paid compliments, and commended on being feminine and beautiful. The '*Fashion Verdict*' episodes broadcast on the last working day prior to this public holiday tend to be especially focused on the issues of femininity and traditional sexuality and gender roles, which makes them particularly relevant to the objective of the research.

Russian anti-LGBTQ legislation serving as a discursive background for the research, the episodes were also selected based on the year of broadcasting: the year when the 'anti-gay-propaganda' law was being discussed and introduced (2013); the year immediately after that (2014); and the year when the collection of media material for the research on the 'Fashion Verdict' was started (2017). Thus, the case study includes the following three episodes:

- 7th March 2013, 'The Case of the Dream Girl';
- 7th March 2014, 'The Case about What a Woman Wants';
- 7th March 2017, 'The Case about a Wedding Dress that Cancelled the Wedding'.

The archived episodes were accessed on the official website of Channel One (https://www.1tv.ru/), and the implementation of Vassiliev's gestures was recorded in the form of screengrabs.

For the purpose of this analysis, a multi-layer approach to identifying, classifying, and analyzing gestures was applied. Individual gestures were selected based on frequency and repetition: three gestures were identified in the three episodes of the "*Fashion Verdict*" show as regularly repeated (either identically or in variations) throughout the length of each show. After that, the gestures were classified as:

- demonstrative or descriptive (Wundt);
- with a discursive of objective meaning (Efron);
- iconic, metaphoric, conduit metaphors (McNeill) or symbolic (Efron).

Then the gestures were analyzed as part of the show narrative and the embodiment of non-heteronormative sexuality and gender performance.

Alexandre Vassiliev's gesture and bodily performance in the makeover show 'Fashion Sentence' reveals a wide variety of gestures and bodily movements. The camera frequently focuses on the close up of the fashion judge, so the viewer can follow and discern every detail of his expressive, artistic gestures. These gestures present a variety of discursive types, including deictic gestures such as a slow waving of the hand and arm when pointing at an object or addressing a person. Another type of gestures frequently applied by the presenter is speech discourse-organizing gestures, e.g., raising hands up into the air when announcing the topic of the episode or drawing his hands close to his chest when addressing the studio audience.

The first brand gesture chosen for analysis is a mixed, multi-purpose type gesture that consists in drawing the thumb and the index finger of the right hand in the shape of the international 'OK' sign, lifting the right hand up to the eye level and then moving the hand slowly towards the large screen hanging in the studio which is used to translate videos during the show (see images 1-3). From the point of view of its functions, this gesture is simultaneously:

- Deictic and demonstrative, as it is used to point at the screen;
- Iconic, as its shape looks similar to a monocle or spyglass;

- Metaphoric, as it symbolizes the act of looking at something closely and carefully;
- Speech discourse-oriented, as by using this gesture Vassiliev monitors and regulates the plot of the show episode. The gesture is used to interrupt the verbal narrative of the communication between the presenters and the participants with a video, i.e., visual piece.

Images 1-3. Screenshots from 'Fashion Sentence' episodes of 7th March 2013 (top left), 2014 (top right) and 2017 (bottom), demonstrating the implementation of the 'monocle/OK' gesture.

In Alexandre Vassiliev's implementation, the international symbolic 'OK' gesture is transformed into a pointing metaphoric gesture used to discursively regulate the narrative of the show, and this transformation itself is a result and embodiment of transgression. The gesture which a Russian viewer would expect in the context of pointing at a screen and signaling that one should watch something very carefully would be either the gesture of raising the index finger in the direction of the gaze (which can be considered impolite, but is a common, widely used gesture); or raising one hand with the palm held straight and open, with the back of the hand moving towards the object or person to look at; or holding a pointer in a hand and raising it towards the screen. By joining his fingers in an imitation of a monocle or a spyglass, Vassiliev adds a theatrical element to his gesture, while also making a historical reference to the times when monocles and spyglasses were commonly used for discerning remote views and objects. It is important to note that the transgression in the case of this gesture is twofold: a culturally accepted and contextually typical deictic gesture is substituted by the 'brand' gesture of the presenter; and at the same time the international 'OK' sign is reinterpreted, with its function and discursive meaning completely altered by Vassiliev.

The second brand gesture observed in all the three show episodes and noticed to be frequently used by Alexandre Vassiliev as another 'brand' gesture of the TV celebrity is a discourse-oriented beat, i.e., a gesture used to rhythmically organize spoken discourse and to accentuate significant bits of information communicated in speech. This gesture consists of the left or right index finger being raised up and is similar to the international sign meaning 'attention' or 'warning' (see images 4-6).

Images 4-6: Screengrabs demonstrating the implementation of the raised index finger beat-gesture

By using this gesture as a beat which organizes spoken discourse, Vassiliev emphasizes important parts of verbally expressed information (e.g., introducing a new section of the show). The implementation of this gesture produces two main effects: on the one hand, this helps create the image of a strict judge, a patriarchal figure who is about to give instructions to the carefully watching and listening audience. On the other hand, the exquisite implementation of the gesture allows Vassiliev to demonstrate his non-heteronormative masculinity – not the stereotypical brutal one, but that of an almost feminine, gentle, stylish, artistic man. The fashion judge raises his finger into the air and the audience in the studio and beyond can observe the large finger rings he is wearing and admire the gracefulness of the gesture. This brand gesture of Vassiliev's demonstrates how two seemingly opposite discursive meanings can be blended in a celebrity's gesticulation. The transgressive gender and sexuality performance of a non-heteronormative male presenter at the same time serves to mediate him as a patriarchal figure that possesses discursive power to regulate or inform the gender and sexuality performance of the makeover show participants and the target audience, e.g., Russian women.

The third example of how Vassiliev uses his brand gestures as part of his non-heteronormative gender and sexuality performance, whereby various individual symbolic gestures refer to a woman's body. For example, in the episode of 7th March 2014, the closing scene shows one of the two suggested outfit sets, usually voted by the studio audience. Vassiliev then announces that the defendant will receive the more attractive outfits prepared by the program stylists without any voting because the whole show crew are impressed by her 'two complete higher educations' (*dva zakonchennykh vyshykh obrazovaniya*). While saying these words, Vassiliev thrusts his hands ahead towards the defendant's chest, both his hands folded in a shape of a woman's breasts (see image 7).

Image 7: A screenshot from a scene of the 2014 episode. Vassiliev to the defendant: "Your two complete higher educations"

It is clear from this gesture that the fashion judge is using a pun here and is referring to the defendant's bosom rather than her level of education: in the Russian language, the noun '*obrazovanie*' stands both for 'education' and 'formation'. The expression 'higher education' (*vysshee obrazovaniye*) is sometimes used to refer to a woman who has attractive big breasts. By thrusting both his hands ahead as if trying to grab the defendant's breasts Vassiliev performs an act of transgression: he challenges the accepted norms of behavior and his gesture can be interpreted as borderline sexual harassment. However, the discursive complexity of this gesture eliminates its interpretation as a sexual harassment attack. Although using this gesture the fashion judge objectifies the defendant, reducing her to an object of male gaze and male desire, Vassiliev's own non-heteronormative performance of a homosexual man signals that his gaze is not that of a sex predator. There is no desire and his gestures are therefore harmless to the defendant. Vassiliev's transgressive gesture objectifies the defendant's body but, at the same time, desexualizes it. By doing so, the fashion judge interrupts the show's narrative and turns the discussion of the defendant's beauty into a joke. This does not challenge the program's overall discourse on heteronormativity and prescribed gender and sexuality norms; on the contrary, the role of a woman as a pleasant object of the male gaze is confirmed.

Conclusion

The analysis presented above reveals that the key discursive value of gendered gesture implemented as part of non-heteronormative gender and sexuality performance is that of transgression. The transgression, in this case takes, place on several levels:

1. As transgression and discursive reinvention of already existing commonly used gestures (e.g., the 'OK/monocle' metaphoric gesture by Vassiliev);

2. As transgression of 'traditional' gender norms through gesture (e.g., the raised index finger gesture performed with feminine gracefulness and demonstrating exquisite ornate finger rings);

3. As transgression of socially accepted norms of gendered behavior (e.g., the breast grabbing gesture).

The case study demonstrates the importance of transgressive non-heternormative brand gestures in the mediation of 'non-traditional' sexuality and gender performance, as well as in sustaining the societally prescribed 'traditional' sexuality and gender discourses within the context of a makeover TV show. Further research into the mediation of non-heteronormative sexuality and gender performance and into the discursive use of transgressive non-heternormative celebrity brand gestures has the potential to revisit and complicate discussions on LGBTQ discourses in contemporary Russian media.

References

Baer, B.J. (2009) *Other Russias. Homosexuality and the Crisis of Post-Soviet Identity*. New York: Palgrave Macmillan.

Butler, J. (2007) *Gender trouble. Feminism and the subversion of identity*. New York and London: Routledge

Christensen, C.L. (2010) Lifestyle as factual entertainment. In: *Relocating television. Television in the digital context.* Ed. by Jostein Gripsrud, Routledge: London and New York, 125-138.

Hall, K., Goldstein, D.M., and Ingram, M.B. (2016) The hands of Donald Trump: Entertainment, gesture, spectacle, *Journal of Ethnographic Theory* 6 (2): 71–100.

Hariman, R. (1995) *Political style: The artistry of power.* Chicago: University of Chicago Press.

Hartley, J. (1999) *Uses of Television.* London: Routledge.

Jannedy, S. and Mendoza-Denton, N. (2005) Structuring Information through Gesture and Intonation, *Interdisciplinary Studies on Information Structure* 03: 199–244

Jolly, S. (2000) Understanding body language: Birdwhistell's theory of kinesics, *Corporate Communications: An International Journal*, Vol. 5 Issue 3, 133-139, https://doi.org/10.1108/13563280010377518

Kadir, S. and Tidy, J. (2013) Gays, Gaze and Aunty Gok. The disciplining of gender and sexuality in How to Look Good Naked, *Feminist Media Studies*, 13(2) 177-191, https://doi.org/10.1080/14680777.2011.604342

Kazakevich, O. (2010) Negotiating citizenship on Russian makeover television: between traditional and neoliberal. *Journal of Siberian Federal University. Humanities and Social Sciences* 1 (9), 55-67. DOI: 10.17516/1997-1370-2016-9-1-55-67

Kendon, A. (2004) *Gesture: Visible Action as Utterance.* Cambridge: Cambridge University Press.

Kolehmainen, M. and Mäkinen (2011) The economics of gay reality television. The visualisation of sexual difference in contemporary consumer culture. In: Stocchetti, M. and Kukkonen, K. (eds.) (2011). *Images in use.* Amsterdam / Philadelphia: John Benjamins Publishing Company, 225-244

Kondakov, A. (ed.) (2014) *Na Pereput'ie. Metodologiia, Teoriia i Praktika LGBT i Kvir-Issledovanii.* Sbornik Stat'ei, Saint Petersburg: Centre for Independent Social Research.

Kress and van Leeuwen (2001) *Multimodal Discourse: The Modes and Media of Contemporary Communication.* Oxford UK: Oxford University Press.

Kosofsky Sedgwick, E. (1990) *Epistemology of the closet.* New York: Harvester Wheatsheaf.

Lovelock, M. (2018) *Gay and happy: (Proto-)homonormativity, emotion and popular culture*, Sexualities, 2018, https://doi.org/10.1177/1363460718758666

McNeill, D. (1992) *Hand and Mind. What Gestures Reveal about Thought.* Chicago and London: The University of Chicago Press.

McNeill, D. (1985) So You Think Gestures Are Nonverbal? *Psychological Review*, 1985, Vol. 92, No. 3, 350-371

Mondada, L. (2016) Challenges of multimodality: Language and the body in social interaction, *Journal of Sociolinguistics*, Vol. 20, Issue 3, 336-366, DOI: doi.org/10.1111/josl.1_12177

Navaretta, C. (2016) Barack Obama's pauses and gestures in humorous speeches, *Proceedings of the 4th European and 7th Nordic Symposium on Multimodal Communication* (MMSYM 2016), ISBN 978-91-7685-423-5,28-36

Persson, Emil (2014) Banning "Homosexual Propaganda": Belonging and Visibility in Contemporary Russian Media, *Sexuality & Culture*, 19(2): 256-274.

Sperling, V. (2015) *Sex, politics and Putin. Political legitimacy in Russia*. New York: Oxford University Press.

Stella, F. (2014) *Lesbian lives in Soviet and Post-Soviet Russia: post/socialism and gendered sexualities*. Basingstoke and New York: Palgrave Macmillan.

Streeck, J. (2008) Gesture in Political Communication: A Case Study of the Democratic Presidential Candidates During the 2004 Primary Campaign, *Research on Language and Social Interaction* 41:2, 154-186, DOI: 10.1080/08351810802028662

Strukov, V. (2017) The Gesture of Alterity. Renata Litvinova and the Mediation of Contemporary Russian Sensibility. In Hashamova, Y., Holmgren, B., and Lipovetsky, M. (eds.) *Transgressive Women in Modern Russian and East European Cultures. From the Bad to the Blasphemous*. Taylor and Francis. Kindle Edition

Turner, G. (2010). *Ordinary people and the media. The demotic turn*. SAGE Los Angeles – London – New Delhi –Singapore – Washington

Wehling, E. (2009) Argument is Gesture War: Function, Form and Prosody of Discourse Structuring Gestures in Political Argument, *Berkeley Linguistics Society Proceedings of the Annual Meeting*, Vol. 35, No 2, 54-65, DOI: http://dx.doi.org/10.3765/bls.v35i2.3511

Wu, Y.C. and Coulson, S. (2015) Iconic Gestures Facilitate Discourse Comprehension in Individuals with Superior Immediate Memory for Body Configurations, *Psychological Science*, 26(11) 1717–1727

Gossip and Persona: Online Gossip and Perceptions of Meghan Markle's Identity Work

Bronagh Allison

Abstract. Celebrity gossip may mirror real-world gossip. Gossip's functions include social learning and reputation management. Online gossip facilitates intense scrutiny of public figures, allowing consumers to learn performative lessons from a celebrity's persona presentation. A case study of one article on Celebitchy.com illustrates the extent of the scrutiny some celebrities face. In Markle's case, this scrutiny speaks to the tension in her public identity as an actor and that of a royal. Gossip's functions in critiquing persona performance and identity creation suggest that while a celebrity is a feature of public social learning, they will face difficulties overcoming negative comments.

Keywords: gossip, persona, Meghan Markle, royals.

Introduction

An American divorcée, mysterious and somewhat aloof, steals the heart of one of the world's most sought-after bachelors, a handsome prince in the British royal family. Although she and her prince enjoy the support of the British public, tensions are brewing with the prince's sister-in-law. The American divorcée is a glamorous woman, presenting herself in the best of fashion, which she uses to project her chosen persona to the watching world. Her glamour and persona are contrasted with the prince's sister-in-law, who is said to be slightly matronly in her public persona and presentation.

Although this reads like the tale of the relationship between Meghan Markle, the Duchess of Sussex, and Kate Middleton, the Duchess of Cambridge, it describes the story of Wallis Simpson, future Duchess of Windsor, and her relationship with the future Queen Elizabeth and the Queen Mother of the British royal family in the 1930s. All four women, although temporally and generationally separated, have been discussed in gossip columns and had their fashion and life choices dissected, and all four have been subject to the hyper-scrutiny that women in the public eye face (Fairclough, 2012).

The primordial human behaviors of gossip and persona and identity creation intersect in the very modern online world. The performance function of gossip as a display of communication skill (Dunbar, 1996) and persona as performative creation (Marshall & Barbour, 2015) can be illustrated in the ways that online gossip sites act as vehicles for the extensive scrutiny of the personas that those in the public eye have created. Although gossip is a behavior that people have engaged in since language became their primary means of communication, through the proliferation of ways to scrutinize those in the public eye, gossip forums have become a vehicle through which celebrities can create and perform their chosen persona.

Theoretical perspectives

Increased media forums since the 1930s have broadened the space for the particular celebrity to create a persona through which consumers of gossip and public figures can negotiate the meaning of celebrity (Widholm & Becker, 2014). Furthermore, celebrity gossip may be a proxy for real-world gossiping (Yao, Scott, McAleer & Sereno, 2014), and gossiping about celebrities online is only a move away from real-world gossip. Online gossip also represents a new way of sharing information that would have been alien to those in the public eye in the 1930s.

For Marshall and Barbour (2015), personas are strategic masks—the façade an individual wears to facilitate performance, the creation of identity, and reputation management. Persona and identity creation are ways to mark how an individual's private face interacts with their public and social identity (Marshall & Barbour, 2015), which, in the case of celebrities may involve a prolific public presence. For Marshall and Barbour (2015), persona has close links to performance and presentation, and celebrities can choose various means through which to present their preferred identity, such as through drama, music, or art.

Meghan Markle is an individual whose public life has occupied two levels of celebrity: an actor with a career that allowed her public visibility; and now as the Duchess of Sussex in the British royal family. Widholm and Becker (2014) suggest that although royalty and royal families help to construct notions of nation and national belonging, they also reflect a version of celebrity that depends on a negotiation between individual, audience, and media involvement in the promotion of the royal celebrity. In that sense, royals are celebrities who are seen through the lens of nationhood.

The shift in public persona that Markle negotiated was achieved previously when Hollywood actor Grace Kelly married Prince Rainier of Monaco. However, Markle is a powerful example of Widholm and Becker's (2014) discussion of how royalty merges celebrity identities. Unlike Kate Middleton, the Duchess of Cambridge, who was widely described as a commoner and had no public profile before her involvement with the royal family, Markle had to learn to construct a new persona as a royal distinct from her identity as a television celebrity.

Just as celebrity construction relies on the involvement of the media to support or attack the individual, the construction of a royal persona involves private roles that will be for and scrutinized by public consumption, channeled by the media. Similar to the now Prince Daniel of Sweden (Widholm & Becker, 2014), public discourse was concerned with how Meghan Markle would receive six months of "princess lessons" to assist with her shift in identity (Proudfoot, 2018). With these princess lessons, Markle would learn how to curtsy, speak at royal occasions, and dress appropriately—all for the performance of her persona as a British royal. Markle's double identity as an actor and royal make her attractive for gossip columnists and bloggers, for whom talking and communicating information about celebrities is a way to hold up the person in the public eye as a yardstick against which the non-celebrity can measure themselves (Fairclough, 2012).

Although Fairclough (2012) considers specifically the aging woman in the public eye, the fashion choices of royal women are also highly scrutinized. For example, the ways in which people such as Markle and Middleton dress or wear their hair are used by gossip columnists as examples of how people should or should not present themselves. Such social learning is an element of the theoretical canon on gossip. Baumeister, Zhang, and Vohs (2004) perceive gossip as a vehicle for cultural learning through which people learn through imitation of how to behave. Cultural and social learning involves learning from others' actions, observing the positive or negative reaction, and determining that that course of action may be one to follow. Furthermore, gossip can be the means by which an individual's reputation rises or falls. For McAndrew and Fisher (2014), an important element of this phenomenon is reputation management— as individuals strive to protect their reputation through the extent to which they have assimilated the learning opportunities in their social world. Celebrity gossip sites are therefore a means for the public to discuss the successes or failures of a given famous person, depending on the subject of the article in which they appear.

In the present study, we will focus on one story as a case study in order to demonstrate how gossip—a tool for social learning and reputation management—can also be a vehicle for an individual's persona creation that allows the public to assess and comment on media forums on the success or failure of the celebrity's performance. Markle's public persona as a blended royal celebrity, the ways in which she has to learn how to perform that persona in the constraints decreed by royal protocol, and the proliferation of spaces— online gossip sites—on which to debate the successes or failures of her identity project, through a public discussion of her efforts, offer a way to gain access to the reception of her new persona as a royal who is shedding her persona as an actor.

Method

The article for this case study concerns persona creation through fashion, focusing specifically on the ostensibly frivolous topic of buttons. The article and the comments on it were analyzed. The article is about an outfit chosen by Markle for one of her first public appearances with the Queen after her wedding to Prince Harry of Wales. Fashion regularly features on the site, and buttons were first used on the celebrity gossip website www.celebitchy.com about the Duchess of Cambridge's clothing in July 2011. Thematic analysis was deemed the most suitable means of accessing public views of Markle's new persona, as people were able to directly view and comment on their perceptions of Markle's identity project. The ways in which they perceive her new persona and how they use it to inform how they see fashion should be used to create her identity are writ large in the comments that emerge.

Results and themes

At the time of writing, there were 315 responses to this story. Twenty stories were published on www.celebitchy.com on 27 June 2018. A person writing under the pseudonym Kaiser, a long-term writer on the website, wrote:

"We were waiting to see what the Duchess of Sussex would wear for her big appearance at Buckingham Palace on Tuesday evening … it seemed like Meghan was trying to follow the Queen's lead. It didn't really work out."

In this quotation, Kaiser is anticipating how the new duchess would construct a persona through her fashion choice for the occasion as a member of the British royal family. The genderized hyper-scrutiny (Fairclough, 2012) reached the level of the duchess's buttons and became a judgment on how the outfit's buttons somehow impacted detrimentally on Markle's ability to create a successful royal persona. Unlike her previous persona, the royal identity is being judged in this article on her clothes and make-up and the minutiae of the buttons on her outfit. Similar to Fairclough's (2012) noting of comments on Nicole Kidman, the intended public persona of the celebrity has been reframed by those judging and commenting on it, with the result that the individual will ultimately fail to please the watching public.

The principal theme that emerged from this article was comparisons between finer details of the buttons on Markle's and Kate Middleton's outfits. Kaiser wrote:

"Meghan is going all-in on buttons. I THOUGHT YOU WERE DIFFERENT, MEG."

This suggests that Markle has failed in her endeavors to carve out a different royal persona than the Duchess of Cambridge. This comment not only judges an early failure of Markle's but puts her in a sartorial competition with her new sister-in-law, where she has to be different to Kate yet somehow similar. Indeed, recent media discussion has put Markle and Middleton in direct competition with each other and has suggested a fractured relationship, mainly reflected in their respective choice of clothing (Adegoke, 2018).

However, the narrative in the article and the readers' comments on the use of buttons mask the underlying work in the article, which is a commentary on the success or otherwise of the Duchess of Sussex's new efforts to adopt a persona suitable for the British royal family. Markle's identity creation is being compared and contrasted unfavorably with the Duchess of Cambridge's, which in turn is negatively discussed. For example, one commenter wrote:

"Katie Keen LOVES big ass shiny buttons".

Another commenter wrote of the buttons:

"I once joked that Kate thought of Meghan as Duchess Buttons-Come-Lately".

Another said:

"People call Kate lazy, but look how much she's done for British Button!"

"Buttons!!! It's the first thing I thought when I saw the pictures."

Furthermore, the Duchess of Cambridge was variously referred to as "Princess of Buttons", and "Queen Buttons".

Discussion

The discussion on buttons reveals that commenters were interested in using them as a device to assess the sartorial choices and public personas of the Duchess of Sussex. These comments on the details of the buttons worn by Meghan Markle reflect how female celebrities are subject to the hyper-scrutiny noted by Fairclough (2012). The absence of commentary on Markle's husband underlines the genderization of her persona and suggests that not only does she have to work harder to create her new persona because she is a woman, but her performance in this role is justifiably open to such scrutiny. The level of discussion on buttons highlights how gossip is used as a vehicle for social learning (Baumeister et al., 2004): these buttons are a public yardstick by which the website's readership can judge their own fashion choices and reflect on how their own identity will be perceived.

These comments in celebitchy.com illustrate one main type of identity and persona work. The royal persona that Markle is trying to create and that Middleton has created are being offered up for scrutiny. Unacknowledged is the tension in Markle's public life: she is shifting from the public persona of actress and "star" to the equally public persona of royal. In Marshall and Barbour's (2015) terms, Markle is having to learn a different type of performance in the gaze of the public eye. Similar to Wallis Simpson, Meghan Markle's identity prior to her involvement with the royal family and her need to blend her identities to perform appropriately under intense scrutiny are deemed suitable material for public gossip. However, the proliferation of media outlets through which the public can both gossip about Markle as a royal celebrity and judge themselves against her standards means the modern duchess may find the most minor elements of her public persona critically assessed.

References

Adegoke, Y. (2018, December 3). The fake feud between Meghan and Kate reveals the prejudice of the press. *The Guardian*. Retrieved from www.theguardian.com

Baumeister, R.F., Zhang, L., & Vohs, K. D. (2004, June). Gossip as cultural learning. *Review of General Psychology*. https://doi.org/10.1037/1089-2680.8.2.11

Dunbar, R. I. M. (1996). *Grooming, gossip, and the evolution of language*. London, UK: Faber and Faber.

De Backer, C.J.S. & Fisher, M.L. (2012). Tabloids as windows into our interpersonal relationships: A content analysis of mass media gossip from an evolutionary perspective. *Journal of Social, Evolutionary, and Cultural Psychology, 6(3)*, 404-424. doi: 10.1037/h0099244

Fairclough, K. (2012). Nothing less than perfect: Female celebrity, ageing and hyper-scrutiny in the gossip industry. *Celebrity Studies*, *3*(1), 90–103. https://doi.org/10.1080/19392397.2012.644723

Gabriels, K. & De Backer, C.J. S. (2016) Virtual gossip: How gossip regulates moral life in virtual worlds. *Computers in Human Behavior*. doi: 10.1016/j.chb.2016.05.065

Kaiser. (2018, June 27). Duchess Meghan got buttony in Prada for an event at Buckingham Palace [Blog post]. Retrieved from https://www.celebitchy.com/582861/duchess_meghan_got_buttony_in_prada_for_an_event_at_buckingham_palace/

Marshall, P. D., & Barbour, K. (2015). Making intellectual room for Persona Studies: a new consciousness and a shifted perspective. *Persona Studies*, *1*(1), 1–12. https://doi.org/10.21153/ps2015vol1no1art464

McAndrew, F. T., & Fisher, M. L. (2014). How "The Gossip" Became a Woman and How "Gossip" Became Her Weapon of Choice, *The Oxford Handbook of Women and Competition* (March), 1–18. https://doi.org/10.1093/oxfordhb/9780199376377.013.13

Proudfoot, J. (2018, May 25). What will Meghan Markel be learning in her six months of Princess lessons? *Marie Claire*. Retrieved from https://www.marieclaire.co.uk

Widholm, A., & Becker, K. (2015). Celebrating with the celebrities: television in public space during two royal weddings. *Celebrity Studies*, *6*(1), 6–22. https://doi.org/10.1080/19392397.2015.995897

Yao, B., Scott, G.G., McAleer, P. & Sereno, S.C. (2014). Familiarity with interest breeds gossip: Contributions of emotion, expectation, and reputation. *PLoS ONE*, *9(8)*. doi: 10.1371/journal.pone.0104916

The Model as (Black) Phallus: Milton Moore, Thomas Williams, and Robert Mapplethorpe

Pete Sigal

Abstract. Thomas Williams's glistening skin emanates from an advertisement in which a black leather briefcase hides one part of his naked body. An advertisement with Milton Moore inverts the Williams ad: the only skin displayed in the Moore ad is that of a large uncircumcised penis extending from the open fly of a polyester suit. This chapter explores the ways in which the two models, both black men, help to formulate photographer Robert Mapplethorpe's position as the celebrity promoting his own brand.

Keywords: Robert Mapplethorpe, race, photography.

When we witness an advertisement in which a black leather briefcase hides a naked man's genitals, we think about those genitals. When we witness another advertisement in which a clothed man's penis sticks out from his suit pants, we think about that penis. Yet, in both cases, the advertisements present us with a puzzle and a provocation: the advertisers intend to sell briefcases and suits, not genitalia. The models become signified through their genitals, and they effectively *become* the phallus: in order to produce a particular type of desire for a brand, the model serves as the phallic signifier for that brand.[1] This essay makes three points: first, photographer Robert Mapplethorpe used the black male body to enhance his fame and develop his brand; second, the images present two African American models, Milton Moore and Thomas Williams, as the (black) phallus, to signify history and desire, and third, the broader world of commercial advertising also uses the (black) phallus and black skin to sell products.[2]

---

[1] The phallus is a sign of desire (for the product, for the man's body, etc.), not the penis itself. Jacques Lacan articulates a theory of the phallus—specifically not the penis or clitoris (Lacan, 2002, p. 579)—as the privileged signifier of all desire, stemming from the child's primary desire for the love and attention of their mother: "If the mother's desire *is* for the phallus, the child wants to be the phallus in order to satisfy her desire" (Lacan, 2002, p. 582).

[2] The parentheses here signify blackness in erasure. The racial structure of the advertisement both mandates the power of blackness to signify desire and denigrates that power through abjection (Scott, 2010; Sharpe, 2016).

Williams and Moore's names remain obscure, while Mapplethorpe has become a celebrity; in effect, after his death, *he* became the brand. Mapplethorpe first became famous through his images of New York City's gay leather community of the 1970s (see Mapplethorpe and Levas, 1999). One of his most iconic images is a self-portrait in which a bullwhip emanates from the photographer's buttocks (Mappethorpe, 1978). His gaze appears to challenge us to read pleasure as he has contorted his body into the most uncomfortable position. The bullwhip moves out of the frame toward the camera. If one thinks about a leather community and a set of sexual acts that form sadomasochism, this shot fails to cohere. What sexual acts could this photograph possibly perform? The image presents Mapplethorpe's open anal cavity staring back at us just like his eyes. Such a challenge, of traditional studio photography with a very queer subject, signifies something centrally important to Mapplethorpe's work. The queer subject here fails to cohere as human and the act depicted in the shot fails to cohere as sexuality, perhaps signifying something monstrous (See Grosz, 1994; Bersani, 1996; Scott, 2010; Sharpe, 2010; Halberstam, 2011; Delany, 2015).

This queer notion of subjectivity plays a similar role in Mapplethorpe's photographs of black men (several scholars have analyzed Mapplethrorpe's treatment of race and his fetishization of black men. See, for example, Mercer, 1994; Mercer and Julien, 1994; Muñoz, 1997; Marriott, 2000; Stockton, 2006; Allen, 2016). An image of Milton Moore, one of Mapplethorpe's most treasured lovers and models, on vacation in Puerto Rico presents a thin man in motion who seems playful, with waves behind him and his blanket fluttering in the air (Mapplethorpe, 1981). Mapplethorpe expressed great affection toward Moore both in this photoshoot and in their life together. At the Mapplethorpe Foundation's offices, I examined the contact sheets for the shoot, where I found an extremely playful Moore—the lovers were having fun. Yet, in Mapplethorpe's studio, in several photo shoots, Moore became the headless sign of racialized hypermasculinity, with a nicely proportioned abdomen, muscly arms and neck, and a large penis. Mapplethorpe saw Moore as the ultimate sign of masculine perfection, something clearly present in "Hooded Man," a full-frontal image in which Moore has his head covered with a hood reminiscent of a Ku Klux Klan hood, and wearing nothing else (Mapplethorpe, 1980a). Moore requested that his face never appears in the same picture with his soon to be famous large uncircumcised penis (Morrisroe, 1995, pp. 245-246). Mapplethorpe and Moore relate a historical phenomenon, the lynching of the black man, with the (black) phallus, so central to the white mobs that lynched, and, at times, castrated, black men (Wiegman, 1995; Allen, 2000). This historical reckoning in the image stands in contrast to the thin, playful man in the Puerto Rican photograph.

In a 1984 lecture, Mapplethorpe states, "The texture of black skin is something that excites me photographically maybe as well as other ways . . . There was a reason that bronzes are bronze. The subtleties of skin tone somehow are more refined" (this lecture is recorded in the Robert Mapplethorpe archive at the Getty Research Institute—henceforth, GRI 2011.M.20, Box 183, f. 3). The fetish of black skin signified for him both sexual desire, similar to his desire for black leather, and a fetishized object that photographed well. Mapplethorpe's gaze and camera capture the perfect statue. The hooded black man with the uncircumcised penis becomes a doubled sign, signifying both racial degradations within history and fetishistic desire within modern sexual pleasure (Stockton, 2006, pp. 103-106). The historical recreation plays with symbols visualized through the photograph—the "big black cock" that has become an object of desire and anxiety, along with the hood, signifying both lack of subjectivity and the representation of terror through its relationship with the KKK (Marriott, 2000). This representation of the "big black cock" becomes so centrally connected to such images that Scott Poulson Bryant notes, as he begins his meditation on black masculinity, that his own "soft hanging dick is not the monster of Mapplethorpean proportions that draws looks of wonder and awe. Of course many men are grow-ers rather than show-ers, but that doesn't mean I'm not still conscious of it . . . partly because I am a black man" (Bryant, 2005, p. 6). Black masculine worth becomes measured through the penis, but also becomes closely connected with lack: of subjectivity and power. The hood that Moore wears signifies the black man's castration: despite the natural fact of the large penis undisturbed by the cultural alteration of circumcision, Moore becomes castrated by history and memory—his most famous images have neither his face nor his name (One may also note Moore's own psychological and legal struggles as represented in the archive. See the letter from Moore to Mapplethorpe in GRI 2011.M.20, box 187).

Moore was the model for "Man in Polyester Suit," a photograph of a man in a three-piece suit, picturing his body from chest to thighs, with the fly of the suit pants open, and a large uncircumcised penis emanating from underneath the suit, with just a bit of a white shirt helping to frame the penis. The only skin we see is on the man's penis and hands (Mapplethorpe, 1980b). In the contact sheets for this photograph, Mapplethorpe had several shots of Moore's erect penis and instead chose to produce the one with the flaccid penis in order to emphasize the fact that it was uncircumcised—and thus undamaged, a representation, for Mapplethorpe, of pure beauty. In the image, the penis flops downward at an angle parallel to Moore's left thumb. The light and shading on the penis emphasize both the veins in the penis and the head peeking out from the hood. The hooded head mimics and brings attention to the lack of a face: Mapplethorpe argued that the buttocks and genitals are effective representatives of the subject in portraiture (Interview of Mapplethorpe in GRI 2011.M.20, Box 183, f. 3).

The Mapplethorpe archive contains a Helmut Lang advertisement, a postcard with an image of Man in Polyester Suit, which claims that Lang is the producer of the "finest suits and menswear since 1986" (See Sigal, 2016, figure 8). How could the designer accrue commercial benefit by connecting this image with Lang suits? Given the historical valence of such an image, how could this phallus, like the finely tailored Lang suit, signify success? The use of this image by Helmut Lang suggests a particular investment by Lang in the *shocking* nature of this type of portraiture. Could Lang get so much play with the less shocking image of Moore on the beach in Puerto Rico? Moore's presence signifies a reckoning of the contradictions in relation to Mapplethorpe's celebrity status, which is largely based on the photographer's fetishization of black leather and black skin.[3] Moore became subsumed within this fetish. The camera focused on the visual economy and history of colonialism and slavery, much more than on Moore's humanity. As Darieck Scott and others have noted, the cultural appropriation of black masculinity in images such as those in the Mapplethorpe corpus relates to the sexual abjection of black male slaves and the corresponding historical erasure of that theme (Scott, 2010, pp. 132-136). This abjection follows from a colonial model in which colonizers both feared and desired the strong bodies of colonized men. Mapplethorpe's work with Moore in the studio shines a light on this process, just as his feelings for Moore allowed him to portray a man in motion, a lover thinking about his beloved.

The black skin of another Mapplethorpe model, Thomas Williams, moves from texture to text in order to promote a brand. Mapplethorpe and Williams develop a campaign that focuses on Williams's skin and cloaked penis. The centerfold image has Williams propped up on an elbow, while in a seductive position that shows his entire naked body. However, a briefcase produced by the Japanese designer of accessories, Tokio Kumagai, hides Williams's genitals (GRI 2011.M.20, Box 139). The (black) phallus signifies a history of colonialism and slavery that creates a fantasy—of the occluded and forbidden. The sexual fantasy, envisioned as the ultimate forbidden sexual desire, of the black man with the white woman or man, shown in the 1975 blaxploitation film, *Mandingo*, had a significant influence on Mapplethorpe (Jack Fritscher,

---

[3] Of course, black leather is the skin of a non-human animal. One of the anonymous readers for this essay suggested that I make this connection more explicit: one type of (human) animal skin is used to sell another type of animal skin. While I do not have space to expand on this point here, I note that both human and non-human animals become marginalized in this process.

personal communication, August 1, 2016). This fantasy in Mapplethorpe's work becomes a sign that enforces a *global desire* for the (black) phallus. The advertisement sells this desire for the (black) phallus in a playful manner that alludes to the forbidden. This image is emblematic of this strategy, in that the black leather briefcase hides what one may presume (based both on the structure of the fantasy and common presumptions about Mapplethorpe's work) to be a giant black penis. The perfectly sculpted body of the black man, the way in which the black skin reflects and glistens in the photograph, is intended to make one want to buy the well-crafted men's fashion accessories, particularly black leather. As Michelle Stephens (2014) has noted, building on Frantz Fanon's work (1967), black skin is central to the development of race and the corresponding investment in sexual desire and degradation. Here the skin/leather connection relates to the fantasy in which black skin becomes a fashionable sign. This fantasy, evoked through a colonialist appropriation of black skin, suggests capitalistic cannibalism in which the Japanese company devours the (black) phallus to sell black skin. While historically, in the development of colonial racial ideologies (Tompkins, 2012), *Europeans* symbolically devoured the colonized peoples, in this case, the cannibalism has become a part of global capitalism, which devours the (black) phallus in order to promote the success of the design.

Mapplethorpe met Thomas Williams, the model in the Tokio Kumagai campaign, in the early 1980s. One of Williams's lovers, Veronica Vera, conjectures that the photographer saw Williams in a gay pornographic film (Veronica Vera, personal communication, October 16, 2016). Williams would become one of Mapplethorpe's most popular models in both his commercial and his artistic work (Terpak and Brunnick, 2016, p. 120). As I have noted elsewhere, Mapplethorpe and Williams create a historical vision of black masculinity that links with a fantasy in which the penis is often veiled. A 1987 spread in *Interview,* a magazine founded by Andy Warhol, features Williams with two white women. The spread, intended to sell the dresses the women wear, places Williams in the nude (GRI 2011.M.20, Box 309). Black skin without clothing becomes the fetish designed to sell clothes.

In one image, Williams stands with the two women (Sigal, 2016, figure 4). The background to the picture is so dark that the black outfits are barely visible—despite the fact that the ostensible purpose of this spread is to sell these outfits. Williams wears nothing, and the photograph pictures full-frontal nudity, though his hands cover his crotch. Perhaps most importantly, we can consider the gaze—all of them have their eyes closed; the visual symbolism suggests that they do not want to see, nor do they want us to see, the black penis. With the clothes fading into the background, the closed eyes, and the hidden penis, what else do Mapplethorpe and the models hide? This image objectifies Williams and teases viewers, perhaps making them desire to see what comes next.

The historical vision portrayed in the *Interview* spread relates to a history of interracial desire and stereotypes.Williams becomes, in this imaginary universe, the black stud, full of hypermasculinity. At the same time Williams never wears clothes in a spread designed to sell clothes. Williams becomes imagined as a being full of illicit interracial desire, seduction, and sexual pleasure, in which he becomes involved in a *ménage à trois* with two white women. Williams's muscular body and his hidden penis become the key story, with two white women playing important roles that could, historically, get the black man lynched.

We must recall the power at play in all of the photo shoots: Mapplethorpe, rather than Moore or Williams, becomes a household name. Mapplethorpe both created and reflected upon a 1970s and 1980s culture that linked black masculinity with the phallus—a world that advertising, film, television, and the internet have made even more dominant in recent times. Many scholars have noted that over the past generation, black men in popular music, television, and film, have evoked hypermasculinity and hypersexuality, witnessed through the ethnographic and pornographic gaze of white men (See McBride, 2005; Johnson, 2017). Only recently have producers of popular culture worked to challenge this image, not by rejecting the theme of hypermasculinity, but rather by putting other, alternative, images of black men in play (See the many examples discussed in Johnson, 2016).

In many ways, we cannot envision Williams and Moore at all—we do not know these two as subjects. However, the (black) phallus exists, with the blackness under erasure, for in our racist society the power of the symbolic (black) phallus becomes untenable. Thus, it becomes just the phallus, without any qualifying adjective, and this signifier creates and maintains desire for the brand, for the product. In this very queer signifying chain, the black subject fails to cohere, just as the (black) phallus becomes the sign of all desire.

References

Allen, J. (2016). A Picture's Worth: Toward Theorizing a Black/Queer Gaze in the Internet Pornutopia. *Nka: Journal of Contemporary African Art, 38-39*, 96-100.

Allen, J. (2000). *Without Sanctuary: Lynching Photography in America.* Santa Fe: Twin Palms Publishers.

Bersani, L. (1996). *Homos.* Cambridge: Harvard University Press.

Bryant, S. (2005). *Hung: A Meditation on the Measure of Black Men in America.* New York: Random House.

Delany, S. (2015) *The Mad Man: Or, the Mysteries of Manhattan* (2nd Ed.). New York: Open Road Media.

Fanon, F. (1967). *Black Skin/White Masks.* New York: Grove Press.

Grosz, E. (1994). Experimental Desire: Rethinking Queer Subjectivity. In J. Copjec (Ed.), *Supposing the Subject.* New York: Verso.

Halberstam, J. (2011). *The Queer Art of Failure.* Durham: Duke University Press.

Johnson, E. (Ed.). (2016). *No Tea, No Shade: New Writings in Black Queer Studies.* Durham: Duke University Press.

Johnson, J. (2017) *Killing Poetry: Blackness and the Making of Slam and Spoken Word Communities.* New Brunswick: Rutgers University Press.

Lacan, J. (2002). The Signification of the Phallus. In B. Fink (Ed. and Trans.), *Écrits* (575-584). New York: Norton.

Mapplethorpe, R. (1978). Self-Portrait, N.Y.C. Retrieved from http://www.getty.edu/art/collection/objects/254562/robert-mapplethorpe-self-portrait-nyc-american-1978/.

Mapplethorpe, R. (1980a). Hooded Man. Retrieved from https://collections.lacma.org/node/2155810.

Mapplethorpe, R. (1980b). Man In Polyester Suit. Retrieved from http://www.getty.edu/art/collection/objects/254454/robert-mapplethorpe-man-in-polyester-suit-american-negative-1980-print-1981/

Mapplethorpe, R. (1981). Milton Moore. Retrieved from https://collections.lacma.org/node/2155802.

Mapplethorpe, R. and Levas, D. *Pictures.* Verona: Arena Editions.

Marriott, D. (2000). *On Black Men.* New York: Columbia University Press.

McBride, D. (2005). *White I Hate Abacrombie & Fitch: Essays on Race and Sexuality.* New York: New York University Press.

Mercer, K. (1994). Reading Racial Fetishism: The Photographs of Robert Mapplethorpe. In K. Mercer, *Welcome to the Jungle: New Positions in Black Cultural Studies* (pp. 171-219). New York: Routledge.

Mercer, K. and Julien, I. True Confessions: A Discourse on Images of Black Male Sexuality. In K. Mercer, *Welcome to the Jungle: New Positions in Black Cultural Studies* (pp. 131-141). New York: Routledge.

Morrisroe, P. (1995). *Mapplethorpe: A Biography.* New York: Random House.

Muñoz, J. (1997). Photographies of Mourning: Melancholia and Ambivalence in Van Der Zee, Mapplethorpe, and *Looking for Langston.* In H. Stecopolous and M. Uebel (Eds.), *Race and the Subject of Masculinities* (pp. 337-358). Durham: Duke University Press.

Scott, D. (2010). *Extravagant Abjection: Blackness, Power, and the African American Literary Imagination.* New York: New York University Press.

Sharpe, C. (2010). *Monstrous Intimacies: Making Post-Slavery Subjects.* Durham: Duke University Press.

Sharpe, C. (2016). *In the Wake: On Blackness and Being.* Durham: Duke University Press.

Sigal, P. (2016). Robert Mapplethorpe: The Commercial Archive and the Sexualization of the Black Male Body. Retrieved from http://blogs.getty.edu/iris/robert-mapplethorpe-the-commercial-archive-and-the-sexualization-of-the-black-male-body/.

Stephens, M. (2014). *Skin Acts: Race, Psychoanalysis, and the Black Male Performer.* Durham: Duke University Press.

Stockton, K. (2006). *Beautiful Bottom, Beautiful Shame: Where "Black" Meets "Queer".* Durham: Duke University Press, 2006.

Terpak, F. and Brunnick, M. (2016). *Robert Mapplethorpe: The Archive.* Los Angeles: Getty Research Institute.

Tompkins, K. (2012). *Racial Indigestion: Eating Bodies in the 19th Century.* New York: New York University Press.

Wiegman, R. (1995). *American Anatomies: Theorizing Race and Gender.* Durham: Duke University Press.

The Role of Celebrity in the Fur Debate

Lindsay Parker

Abstract. This paper explores the impact that celebrity personas have had on the fur debate both as promotors of fur and supporters of anti-fur campaigns. The ways in which celebrities' own persona branding have been aligned with and used for the structuring of arguments both for and against the material can reflect wider changing attitudes. As such, celebrities' sustainable lifestyle personas could be used to promote anti-fur sentiment in the future.

Keywords: fur, celebrity, ethical consumption, sustainability.

Introduction

The celebrity persona has long been a central figure within the fur debate with both anti-fur organizations and fur brands utilizing famous faces to sway public opinion on a much debated and often highly controversial topic. The grim realities of the acquisition of fur pelts have long been masked by its association with status and fame, never more so than during Hollywood's golden era. The material has been used lavishly both on and off screen to create a sense of exclusivity and extravagance. This pairing is perhaps best exemplified in Blackglama furs' iconic "What becomes a legend most?" campaigns that utilized the allure of film stars such as Lauren Bacall and Bette Davis. Featuring regal black and white images of fur swathed icons, the advertisements served to highlight the association of the material with glamour and celebrity to the mutual benefit of both the brand and the 'legends' featured.

Despite this erstwhile successful combination, as environmental movements gained momentum in the 1960s and 70s, and the use of animal pelts for fashion began to be challenged by campaign groups, celebrity spokespeople became central to the dissemination of the anti-fur rhetoric. As famous faces were called upon to disparage the trade, a notably effective example was the reinvention of Brigitte Bardot's persona branding from sultry film star to protector of vulnerable baby seals. The image of the star cuddling a wide-eyed baby seal became representative of campaigns against Canadian seal hunts encouraging public support for the cause as well as serving to reposition Bardot's image within the public eye (Nadeau, 2001).

Also utilizing the power of the celebrity persona, People for the Ethical Treatment of Animals (PETA) went on to have a significant impact on the fur trade in the 1980s and 90s. Celebrities were enlisted for hard-hitting campaigns that highlighted gruesome farming conditions and inhumane treatment in order to revoke the material's glamorous associations. PETA understood that as arbiters of popular taste, celebrities can become instrumental in determining wider attitudes towards the uses of animal products in fashion garments. The image of supermodels such as Christy Turlington and Claudia Schiffer baring all in support of the organization and declaring that they would "rather go naked than wear fur" aligned the sex-appeal and glamour of these stars with the animal rights cause. This format has since been repeated frequently by the group, with appearances from a variety of famous faces from the worlds of fashion, music, film, and sport. Not content with focusing only on those who supported their cause, the group also became known for shaming celebrities known to wear fur through targeted campaigns, such as their "worst dressed" list and public flour bombings. As a result, fur sales plummeted and public opinion swayed. Celebrities lined up to present themselves as animal-friendly.

The initial impact of these campaigns, though, was short-lived as fur began to appear on catwalks once again with increasing frequency from the late 1990s onwards. Backlash grew from some defiant designers and celebrities who refused to relent to protests. Prestigious models such as Naomi Campbell and Cindy Crawford, who once campaigned against fur, could be seen advertising luxury fur brands. These brands drew on the persona branding of such icons to once again align fur with glamour, status, and exclusivity. Such dramatic shifts in allegiance can certainly be seen to undermine the success of PETA's celebrity campaigns, suggesting that they no longer had the same clout. The image of fur began to shift again as the fur industry regrouped and rebranded, with the celebrity persona as a key tool in driving this change.

A New Image for Fur?

It is possible that such virulent opposition to the trade may have had the adverse effect of fur becoming "the costume of the rebel, the independent-minded woman who will not be told what to do or think by bothersome, bossy animal activists" (Sorenson, 2011, p.157). Where once it was claimed that models, such as Elle Macpherson (who later did go on to work with Blackglamma), were afraid to appear in fur advertisements because of the assumed backlash from animal rights groups (Moodie, 2005), other celebrities became increasingly defiant in the face of continued criticism.

This association with rebellion is perhaps best exemplified by Kate Moss' determined refusal to comply with activists. The Telegraph reported in 2010 that the resurgence in second-hand fur could be attributed to Moss being frequently seen "out and about in vintage fur, wearing it with the rock and roll insouciance for which she is famous" (Picardie, 2010). Moss' influence on fashion has long been established and her reputation as a rebel cemented by stories of her personal life, which are always closely followed by the press. Reportedly, when questioned about wearing fur, she retorted "I wear what I want to wear" (Fur - the fake debate, 2004). Perhaps Moss was reflecting the attitude of a generation that has grown up with the anti-fur movement and tired of its message. Moss' rebellious persona, therefore, in defiance of anti-fur campaigns, served to give fur a new meaning yet again.

The fur industry swiftly aligned with this counter argument of 'choice'. On their website, wearefur.com, the International Fur Trade Federation (IFTF) has been keen to highlight other celebrity fur wearers and to demonstrate, through their example, that to wear fur is to exercise the right to consume. When Lady Gaga reportedly responded to pleas from PETA to ditch the fur with a firm "I respect your views, please respect mine," IFTF claimed that "Gaga made it clear that the intolerance displayed by anti-fur campaigns had no place in free conversations about society, equality and politics" (Yeates, 2017). Gaga's response to campaigners is very much in keeping with her persona branding as a promoter of individualism and freedom of choice. Through this response, though she is not actively promoting fur, the industry has been able to align her values with their own.

Gaga's response can also be likened to wider changing attitudes. As the fashion-buying public becomes increasingly aware of myriad environmental and ethical issues surrounding the production and consumption of fashion, determining what constitutes "ethical fashion" has become more complex. The fur industry has endeavored to promote itself as a natural, renewable and sustainable resource in order to strengthen their counter argument. Consumers can choose to favor natural fur products over synthetic and environmentally damaging faux fur alternatives. This, however, disregards the toxic chemicals involved in the processing of real pelts (Sorenson, 2011).

Ethical Fur?

The International Fur Trade Federation has sought to highlight the environmental damage caused by the production of synthetic furs and, at the same time, position real fur as a sustainable product by claiming that the industry "helps towards managing eco-systems" (International Fur Trade Federation, n.d). In 2007, IFTF introduced its Origin Assured label in order to "heighten awareness about ethically sourced fur" (Origin assured, 2009, p.80). The label was promoted in a range of advertisements featuring quotes from established designers such as Roberto Cavalli to reassure consumers that by purchasing Origin Assured fur, "they are making a stylish responsible choice" (ibid.). This allusion to a savvy consumer, who wishes to make informed choices about their purchases, is in keeping with a growing discourse of ethical consumption.

Research into motivations behind ethical consumption has identified a range of different approaches and decision-making factors, including reducing consumption, boycotting certain products, and selective and considered purchasing decisions. It is this disparity in individual's interpretation of ethical consumption which the fur industry has targeted. Barnett et al., for example, point to "virtue ethics" in which the focus is on living a positive lifestyle. To these consumers, "moral integrity is more fundamental...than either a concern for consequences or rules" (2005, p.24). This is useful to consider in regards to the seeming decline in influence of PETA's celebrity campaigns. Consumers could be more likely to respond to brands or products that allow them to buy into the 'good life', and to feel that they are making positive consumption choices rather than to be dissuaded from purchases by 'rules' set out by animal rights groups. The discerning consumer may wish to weigh up several issues such as sustainability of the product and environmental impact of the production process.

Rinaldi and Testa describe a "Neo-consumer" who espouses a lifestyle of health and sustainability. This consumer takes care over their consumption choices with consideration for the "quality and origin of the products" (Rinaldi & Testa, 2015, p13). This does not mean that they wish to boycott fashion but rather to feel that they have made informed choices about their purchases by weighing a range of factors (p. 14). The fur industry has been able to capitalize on this, as consumer understanding of the environmental impact of mass consumption has grown; its strategy has been to promote fur as a 'natural' and 'biodegradable' product. By highlighting celebrities who 'choose' to wear fur, they aim to strengthen their claim as a viable, sustainable option.

Sustainable Lifestyle Personas

Although it may appear that the impact of celebrity-led anti-fur campaigns has dwindled, celebrities and their personas could continue to be beneficial for campaign groups as role models for ethical consumption choices. An example of this can be seen in the growing popularity of vegan diets and values, which Julie Doyle argues can be linked to vegan celebrities advocating the lifestyle. According to Doyle "the ethics of veganism are reworked through the commodity logic of celebrity culture" in order to become "more marketable and thus consumable as a set of ideas and lifestyle practices" (2016, p.788). Much like eco-fashion, veganism has seen a change in image. Where once it was linked to a certain stereotype, its associations have broadened to become more accessible and fashionable.

Alicia Silverstone of *Clueless* fame is an example of a celebrity role model that has built a personal brand on advocating a "Kind Life". By producing online content and publishing books through which fans can access detailed information about her lifestyle and emulate the "Kind Life" which she promotes, Silverstone demonstrates an alternative way that consumers can buy into a celebrity lifestyle. Central to her persona branding is the presentation of ethical glamour. This is focused on sustainability and environmental concern rather than status symbols and exclusivity but importantly still appears desirable.

Lagerwey suggests that most successful celebrities spread their personas across platforms in order to "offer access or the illusion of access to a performer's 'real self'" (2017, p.2). By sharing intimate details of her day to day life through a variety of means, Silverstone portrays a covetable lifestyle while still promoting the value of veganism and animal rights. Through her "Kind Life" blog she aligns herself with animal rights organizations such as PETA and outlines her attitude towards both real and faux fur. Guest blogs from other vegan celebrities such as Mena Suvari provide readers with advice to "veganize" their wardrobe, recommending specific clothing brands and faux fur options (The Kind Life, n.d).

Conclusions

The ethics of use of fur in fashion is constantly under debate. Celebrity persona branding has been a key feature throughout its changing reputation and continues to both reflect and influence wider attitudes. Where the fur industry has aimed to reinvent its image by aligning itself with rebellious and free-spirited public figures, campaign groups such as PETA continue to use shock tactics and provocative images of celebrities to elicit support. It is possible however that celebrity-led anti-fur campaigns, relying on a simplistic right and wrong message, may no longer be appropriate. Ethical consumers, rather than rejecting consumption or acting through guilt, look for something positive that they can buy into.

Celebrity lifestyles continue to be sought after and the information that they provide can encourage consumption of certain goods. Celebrity supporters of anti-fur campaigns may have more impact by aligning their persona branding and their rejection of fur with leading a sustainable lifestyle. This approach presents a more compelling argument by conveying an ethically glamourous lifestyle which conscious consumers could adhere to.

References

Barnett, C., Cafarro, P., Newholm, T. (2005). Philospophy and Ethical Consumption. in Harrison, R., Newholm, T., Shaw, D. (Eds.), *The Ethical Consumer* (pp.11-24). London: Sage.

Doyle, J. (2016). Celebrity vegans and the lifestyling of ethical consumption. *Environmental Communication*. 10(6),777-790.

Fur- the fake debate. (2004, November 23). Retrieved from http://www.independent.co.uk/news/uk/this-britain/fur-the-fake-debate-534303.html

International Fur Trade Federation (n.d). Responsible Fur. Retrieved from https://www.wearefur.com/responsible-fur/environment/environmental-impact

Lagerwey, J. (2017). *Postfeminist Celebrity and Motherhood: Brand Mom*. New York, NY: Routledge.

Moodie, C. (2005, September 20). Elle 'too scared' for fur. Evening Standard. Retrieved from https://www.standard.co.uk/showbiz/elle-too-scared-for-fur-7258009.html

Nadeau, C. (2001). *Fur Nation: From the Beaver to Brigitte Bardot*. London: Routledge.

Origin Assured (2009 November). Label Me [Advertisement]. Vogue, New York, 199(11), 79-82.

Picardie, J.(2010, January 7). Why fur is fashionable again. The Telegraph. Retrieved from https://www.telegraph.co.uk/lifestyle/7005774/Why-fur-is-fashionable-again.html

Rinaldi, F.R, Testa, S. (2015) *The Responsible Fashion Company: Integrating Ethics and Aesthetics in the Value Chain*. Sheffield: Greenleaf Publishing.

Sorenson, J. (2011). Ethical fashion and the exploitation of nonhuman animals. *Critical Studies in Fashion & Beauty*, 2 (1&2), 139-164.

The Kind Life. (n.d.). Mena Veganizes Her Closet. Retrieved from http://thekindlife.com/blog/2018/05/mena-veganizes-her-closet/

Yeates, O. (2017, August 1). Celebrities believe in the beauty of fur than flashy PR campaigns [Blog post]. Retrieved from https://www.wearefur.com/celebrities-more-real-fur-than-fake/

Part II:
Style in Ethical Influencer Marketing

Is an Ethics of Bodily Inclusion Emerging in the Glamorous World of Fashion Models?

Vitor Sérgio Ferreira

Abstract. Recent structural changes in the fashion industry have produced transformations in the forms of embodiment socially valued by the modeling industry. These transformations seem to move in the direction of the democratization of the models' appearance canon, and towards the diversification of corporeality welcomed in the fashion market. Drawing from this perspective, the objective of this article is to comprehend sociologically the conditions, meanings and some of the effects of those changes in a way that can point to the emergence of a new ethics that values inclusive forms of embodiment inside the glamorous and highly selective world of fashion models. The discussion will be empirically based on a set of semi-directed interviews conducted with a set of professional fashion bookers, as well as focus groups done with young fashion models.

Keywords: Fashion models, body, bodily capital, inclusion.

Introduction

A broad definition of what constitutes ethical behavior in fashion goes beyond the sustainability concerns with material goods and processes, and also starts to embrace concerns with the human rights of the consumers and labor force. In this sense, the glamorous and highly selective world of fashion models is being confronted with a variety of human rights concerns, including at the level of social inclusion and representativeness of bodily diversity. Bodily appearance is one of the most important forms of capital in the modeling and fashion industries and requires professional models to embody certain forms of socially valued corporeality (Mears & Finlay, 2005; Soley-Beltran, 2012).

Recent structural changes in the fashion industry have produced transformations in the forms of embodiment that are socially valued to access a career in the modeling industry. These transformations move toward a certain democratization of the models' appearance canon and toward the diversification of the morphology of physical capital welcomed in the fashion market. The "right look" to be a model is not as strict as it was in the past. The ideals of bodily perfection and beauty embodied by the social figure of *top model* are being replaced by common bodies of *real people,* as well as by bodies with physical characteristics that used to be barred at the entrance of the fashion industry in the past (disabilities, tattoos, gender fluidity, maturity, plus-size, ethnicity/race, etc.).

This shift is socially significant because the bodily surface of a fashion model, being a celebrity-icon, "is an aesthetic structure whose sensuous qualities command attention and compel attachment" (Alexander, 2010: 324), triggering the absorption of a moral structure that promotes the understanding that fashion goods and the fashion world can be for everyone. From this point of view, this shift raises a number of relevant questions: are we dealing with new ethical standards inside the fashion industry that value inclusive forms of fashion models' embodiment? Or is this simply a readjustment of the fashion world to the economic crisis, and thus to the lack of capital circulating within it, leading to an opening of its borders and goods towards more diversified bodies?

In order to answer these questions, this article will explore findings from a research project about why and how young people are making a new dream job in the fashion and modeling industry come true.[1] This project sought to examine from a sociological perspective the transitions of young people in Lisbon, Portugal, into new attractive professional worlds, such as being a tattoo artist (Ferreira, 2014), football player, chef, DJ (Ferreira, 2017) and, for purposes of this article, a career as fashion model.

With this aim in mind, I started my fieldwork conducting five interviews with "gatekeepers" from the world of fashion modeling - including directors of modeling agencies and bookers - in order to understand the institutional structure, requisites, and perceptions of the attractiveness of a career as fashion model to young people. The findings explored in this article rely mainly on this set of exploratory interviews. However, this research also draws on interviews conducted with two focus groups comprised of eight young models (five women and three men), and 17 individual interviews with young models in different stages of their career (aged 19 to 34 years old). The fieldwork was carried out between 2013 and 2015.

Being a fashion model as a *new dream job*

It is consensual among all the interviewees that, in recent years, the dreams and aspirations of young people in Portugal to become a fashion model have

[1] "Making dream jobs come true: transitions to new attractive professional worlds to young people", is a research project funded by the Foundation for Science and Technology (PTDC/CS-SOC/122727/2010), coordinated by Dr. Vitor Sérgio Ferreira. For further information, see http://newdreamjobs.wixsite.com/dreamjobs/home-page

been growing. As one head booker noted, until the 1990s, "There were very few models. It's not like now, that everybody wants to be a model! (...) Particularly, for the last three years, it's crazy! It's crazy! It's crazy, because everyone thinks they can be a model!"

This observation indicates the recognition of fashion model as a "new dream job" among younger generations, i.e., as part of the more recent forms of "aspirational labor" (Duffy, 2017), representing the combination of the ideal of getting paid to do what one loves, with the promises of contemporary celebrity cultures: success, glamour, fortune and social visibility while *being oneself* (Sternheimer, 2015).

In fact, the investment in a modeling career is driven by a social belief that the young person can succeed to be *some-body* in the world, providing him or her a feeling of achievement as an individual *and* as a worker. In other words, a sense of individuality which is very difficult to obtain via the types of jobs usually available to young people. In the contemporary labor market, the young are usually perceived as one more amongst many, placed in the backstage of the social scene, and left at the mercy of various mechanisms that submit young people to the invisibility of underemployment, unemployment or the desolating and not promising job. Thus, to become a fashion model is perceived as a way of styling and branding an individual existence in a very self-distinctive way in the youth world.

The current aspirational boom for being a fashion model among young people in Portugal has its roots in the intense growth of the textile industry in Portugal during the 1990s, together with the establishment and expansion of the fashion world as a professional system of collective action. A set of occupations achieved the status of professions, such as stylist and fashion designer, fashion photographer, event producer, fashion journalist, fashion blogger or Instagrammer, etc. The occupation of a fashion model also became increasingly professionalized, mainly due to the appearance of a new range of modeling agencies in the 1990s (Macedo, 2007).

If, until recently, the fashion model was waiting to be chosen directly and individually by the client, they are now more likely chosen, placed and promoted in the market by professional agencies, who have increasingly come to play a structuring role in regulating the world of fashion models. This role starts with the selection process and also includes recruitment, training, and management careers at the national and international levels. Inside each agency, the *bookers* have become the fundamental "tastemakers" of the looks and beauty canons that come to be relevant in the larger world of fashion modeling (Mears, 2011, pp.121-137). In this way, bookers come to act as gatekeepers of that world, managing the contact between the agency's portfolio of models and the potential customers.

In this new organizational context, more and more teenagers have begun looking to embrace a career as a fashion model, either as a full-time career or as a part-time job running parallel to other labor force or educational activities. As one agency director noted,

> The truth is that in the past there weren't so many agencies. (...) [Recently] many agencies have opened up. And that has meant looking for more models. (…) In the old days, there wasn't so much looking for models as there is today. Today, there are people ... at the door of a school, looking for kids, and everyone else ... constantly! In the old days, it didn't happen that way. (...) It was pretty much that [the growth of agencies], which came to make it that way.

Alongside this process of agency expansion, the recent appeal of a career in fashion modeling also results from the increasing media coverage of the activity (Schmitz, 2018; Pereira, 2009). The *mediatization* of the modeling world through contests and reality shows with young contestants, ordinary young people from different backgrounds with diverse life stories and bodily morphologies, has had a transformative effect on the ways audiences have come to imagine access to the world of modeling.

The practice of fashion modeling has become an enchanted occupation, wrapped up in an aura of glamour and celebrity for its protagonists, where anybody who shows "talent" or is willing to "work hard" can dream or aspire to achieve to be in the spotlight (Allen & Mendick, 2012; Mendick, Allen, & Harvey, 2015). As one director of a school for modeling and acting noted,

> It's the TV. That is the main factor responsible for all this. (...) There are young people of thirteen, fourteen years old who believe in it and they think it's possible to make this life and that's what they want. (...) It's to show up, what they want ... (...) [They say] "oh dear! I Love Tyra Banks. I watched America's Next Top Model, I watched that every day, and then they took pictures", and whatever... It's the TV shows. That's just it.

During a focus group, Clara and Jessica, both in the beginning of a fashion modeling career, shared the same opinion, adding weight to the argument for the socialization power of mainstream media and the contemporary power of social media sites such as Instagram and Facebook:

> [Clara] I think television is a medium that provides a lot of information, increasingly, holds the attention of a lot of young people and creates great illusions.

Expectations! [kept saying Jessica]

Yes! [replied Clara] Expectations and illusions. (…) Sometimes this happens with everybody who likes a lot of what they watch on TV and they want to be a model and whatever… And then they want to participate in those contests, like Elite Model Look. (...) And social media have also contributed to the growth of this desire.

From *top model* to *real people*

The widening of dreams and aspirations for fashion modeling is a consequence not only of the growth of agencies dedicated to the recruitment of models, but also of the diversification of areas in which they start to act, with a more permeable access for "real people," the terminology of the fashion world for people with ordinary faces, bodies and silhouettes. In fact, as a response to the exponential growth of work that was required on several fronts, and to the need of different types of faces and silhouettes, there was a great enlargement of the volume and variety of modeling work profiles. This expansion meant that the modeling activity is far beyond the activity of the *editorial models,* as recalled by Mears (2011, pp. 37-45), in the most prestigious runways and relevant fashion shows and editorials, and non-traditional models are hired for the most prestigious advertising campaigns of specific brands. As a booker of one agency stated,

> There are many kinds of agencies that, suddenly, in the last two years, have opened. They are also agencies for actors and extras, agencies working more in the advertising market, even because of what the customer asks them, that is 'real people', that is ordinary people.

Furthermore, in contemporary times of global and radicalized economic crisis, the more traditional market segment for editorial models – that is, the shows and fashion events – has sharply contracted. As a result, job opportunities for the more "traditional" runway model have also contracted. In general, editorial models are models with edgy physical traits that set them apart from "real people". During the time ruled by top models or supermodels, it used to be very tall and skinny women and men, drawn from the more traditional canon of "beauty" and "bodily perfection."

In this context of compression of the fashion shows market, the activity of many modeling agencies started turning to the field of advertising and commercial events, where the ideals of bodily perfection represented by the figures of top or editorial model have little penetration and dissemination. As one booker stated,

> Many years ago, about twenty years ago, there was a model ... The model was the typical model, maybe today we have that image: it was a beautiful model... Today the model is no longer that typical model. Anyone nowadays can enroll in an agency. That's exactly because as I said earlier: there are several areas. 20 years ago, there was only one type of model. The model was a tall model, a model who did runway, a skinny model. Nowadays, no. And in the past that model was also the one making commercials. Nowadays ... what one is looking for, what our clients are looking for in advertising, is a beautiful person, but real. A person who doesn't have that typical air of the old model, but a normal person.

After the economic crisis, the figure of the traditional top model is no longer aligned with market demand – which has fewer possibilities to pay – as well as the unfeasible dreams of aspiring models, considering the body canon represented by that figure. Shifting to the publicity of commercial mass consumption goods, the modeling agencies began to respond to the call of the market to use more images of "ordinary bodies," for easier communication and immediate identification with the consumer. In this way, the fashion world starts to give a public stage to the *commercial model*, the one that displays the normative standards of everyday bodies and shapes.

The *commercial model* is one who works in commercials for common products and brands (mobile phones, food, beverages, etc.), in small events organized for the general public (in shopping malls, for local authorities), or for the promotion of certain brands of mass consumption. This type of model is represented by persons whom the general public easily identifies with and/or identifies on the screen (in the case of being a public person, even without being from the fashion world, as it often happens in Portugal, with actors or micro-celebrities from reality shows).

Therefore, the mediatization of "real people" diversifies and extends the space of bodily possibilities for the exercise of modeling, and also provides a certain "democratization" on the social and bodily spectrum of young people aspiring to enter the profession. At the same time, there is also a profound transformation of the criteria of social and bodily recruitment at the level of the editorial models, in the direction of the enlargement of the morphologies of bodily capital; also at this high level of the modeling practice, we see the entrance of "real people," not in the sense of "ordinary people," but of people with bodily characteristics that used to be barred at the entrance of fashion industry in the past.

In the past, the branded singularity of an editorial model was based on a rare, perfect and beautiful body, as evidenced by the bodies of global top models.

Nowadays, the situation is different: an editorial model is physically requested to have "unusual" or "weird" bodily characteristics, as being an androgenous, drag, having physical characteristics as vitiligo or extensive tattoos, or having disabilities such as being an amputee or having muscular dystrophy, for example.[2]

As one booker put it, the editorial models

> Are the strangest. In fashion, when we are talking about real fashion, they are the strangest. They are the giraffes of the school, the ones that are known [and bullied] as being too tall (...) For example, if we go to Haute Couture, we need to have nine heads [a Portuguese expression meaning to stand above the crowd]. (...) So, there are [different] markets. We have totally contrasting customers, attention! We have customers who only like strange models – what we call the "gremlins" almost, right? -- that make fabulous fashion pictures and images to fashion editorials or ... This is what is more worth in the book of a model, an editorial. And then there's the customer who is fully commercial. For the shirt with flowers, the bath towel...

Conclusion

The arguments made in this paper point to the ethical changes in what is happening in the fashion industry. On one hand, we are clearly dealing with mechanisms of socio-economical exploration, as we know that the bodily democratization of the world of fashion models is happening because of a lack of capital flowing in the fashion market (considering that newcomers arriving earn much less than models in the past, and have much shorter trajectories inside the profession). On the other hand, and at the same time, we are dealing with an opportunity to give visibility and voice to the circulation inside the fashion industry of certain kinds of political discourses on the representation, recognition, and empowerment of social categories traditionally left out of the industry.

This situation can provide new ethical standards related to social and bodily inclusion and diversity in the highly selective and elitist world of modeling. The non-profit organization *Models of Diversity*[3], for instance, is an exemplary

---

[2] As Jamie Brewer, Madeline Stuart or Jilian Mercado, for example, the model who was the star of Diesel's 2014 campaign, and that was signed to IMG Models, the same agency as Gisele Bündchen.

[3] See http://www.modelsofdiversity.org/

case of a social movement that aims at greater diversity in the models we see every day, calling on the fashion, beauty and marketing industries to recognize the beauty in people of all races, ages, shapes, sizes, and abilities.

Are we dealing with a new ethics inside the fashion industry that values inclusive forms of embodiment? Maybe, as the request for all kinds of "real people" does represent "some increase" in the plurality of bodies used for modeling, showcased that the fashion industry is slowly becoming more inclusive of representations of people from an expanding diversity. If, at the end of the day, the overall fashion modeling industry still has a long way to go, there are certainly efforts being made to finally be more inclusive, thereby fostering the empowerment and self-esteem of many social segments that started to have some cultural and social visibility inside and through the world of fashion modeling.

Acknowledgments

This work is financed by national funding from FCT – Fundação para a Ciência e a Tecnologia, I.P. in the scope of the project UID/SOC/50013/2019

References

Allen, K., & Mendick, H. (2012). Keeping It Real? Social Class, Young People and 'Autheticity' in Reality TV. *Sociology*, 47(3) 460–476.

Alexander, J. C. (2010). The Celebrity-Icon. *Cultural Sociology*, 4 (3) 323-336.

Duffy, B. E. (2017). *(Not) getting paid to do what you love: gender, social media, and aspirational work*. New Haven: Yale University Press.

Ferreira, V. S. (2014). Entre as Belas-Artes e as Artes de Tatuar: Novos Itinerários de Inserção Profissional de Jovens Tatuadores em Portugal. *Antropolítica*, (37) 79-106.

Ferreira, V. S. (2017). Being a DJ is not just Pressing the Play: The Pedagogization of a New Dream Job. *Educação & Realidade*, 42 (2) 473-494.

Macedo, A. (2007). *Manequins, agências & companhia*. Porto: Campo das Letras.

Mears, A. (2011). *Pricing beauty. The making of a fashion model*. Berkeley: University of California Press.

Mears, A., Finlay, W. (2005). Not Just a Paper Doll: How Models Manage Bodily Capital and Why They Perform Emotional Labor. *Journal of Contemporary Ethnography*, 34 (3) 317-343.

Mendick, H., Allen, K., & Harvey, L. (2015). 'We can Get Everything We Want if We Try Hard': Young People, Celebrity, Hard Work, *British Journal of Educational Studies*, 63(2) 161-178.

Pereira, C. S. (2009). Representações do Mundo da Moda na Mídia: Do Luxo ao Lixo. *Revista Famecos*, (40) 97-104.

Schmitz, D. M. (2018). O Desejo Juvenil de ser Modelo Profissional e a Mediação da Mídia: Uma Articulação Desde o Aporte de Martín-Barbero. *Intertexto*, (43) 206-222.

Soley-Beltran, P. (2012). Muñecas que Hablam. Ética y Estética de los Modelos de Belleza en Publicidad y Moda. *Revista de Dialectología y Tradiciones Populares*, 67(1) 115-146.

Sternheimer, K. (2015). *Celebrity culture and the American dream: stardom and social mobility*. New Your: Routledge.

Tsaliki, L; Frangonikolopoulos, C. A.; Huliaras, A. (2011*). Transnational celebrity activism in global politics: changing the world?* Bristol: Intellect.

Warner, H. (2013). Fashion, Celebrity and Cultural Workers: SJP as Cultural Intermediary. *Media, Culture & Society*, 35(3) 382-391.

Transmedia, Branding, and Celebrities

Cátia Ferreira and Ana Flora Machado

Abstract. One of the emerging strategies for content production is transmedia. We would like to argue that it is already possible to witness the extension of transmedia logics and strategies to celebrity culture. In order to achieve this goal we will present a case study of the Kardashians, based on content analysis, aiming to demonstrate how they are consolidating their role as celebrities, brand, and influencers through the use of transmedia strategies.

Keywords: branding, celebrities, ethics, Kardashians, transmedia.

Introduction

The contemporary media systems are under reconfiguration and media content tend to be created for different platforms. From the celebrity culture point of view, this change brings new challenges but also new opportunities. One of the emerging strategies for media content production is transmedia storytelling, a strategy that has been applied to areas such as entertainment, marketing, and branding or journalism, and we would like to argue that it is already possible to witness the extension of transmedia logics and strategies to celebrity culture. Based on a qualitative methodology of content analysis of collected data, the chapter presents an overview of the use of transmedia strategies by the Kardashians. The chapter particularly aims to demonstrate how the Kardashians are consolidating their role as celebrities, brand, and influencers, as well as to understand how these strategies are being used to communicate more ethical messages, making audiences aware of serious questions.

The Kardashian-Jenner as a Transmedia World

Commonly known as The Kardashians, the Kardashian-Jenner family has been increasing in reputation and media attention worldwide since the family was invited to star in their reality TV series, *Keeping Up with the Kardashians* (*KUWTK*) in 2007. *KUWTK* has accompanied the growth of the Kardashian-Jenner sisters into adulthood, portraying the manifold expansion of their business ventures and family. However successful *KUWTK* has become over the years, it served primarily to increase the Kardashians' popularity and network growth by making audiences acquainted with the business ventures, social media profiles and spinoffs, which were added later on, creating a synergy between different platforms. Concurrently, this process familiarized the audience with different family members, isolating their image from each other. The universe thus sprung from a variety of online and television content, the former, having been fundamental to their increased popularity. We analyze how the Kardashian-Jenner family's business model is based on transmedia strategies to promote their popularity and ventures. In order to test these premises, we propose to look at this universe through the seven principles proposed by Jenkins (2009).

In 1991, Marsha Kinder used the concept transmedia for the first time to characterize the presence of a fictional franchise in different media in order to build up the audience's loyalty. Nowadays, transmedia concerns the presence in different media, but also the way that presence is managed (Leavenworth, 2011). Transmedia storytelling was proposed by Henry Jenkins (2003, 2006). Jenkin's seven attributes provide understanding of transmedia storytelling and how its different dimensions are articulated. The majority are presented as binomial, contrasting different content productions and, consequently, user experiences that may occur in the same universe. The first is spreadability and drillability, the former concerning the audience's ability to participate in the distribution of different content, and drillability comprehending audiences' will to drill down deeper once it finds content of its preference. The 'hashtagged' category #KUWTK on the website *Wattpad*, where fans engage in narrative writing and roleplaying activities, provides room for a more significant narrative expansion by the fans, where they engage and explore with different worldbuilding experiences. The second principle is continuity and multiplicity: continuity is a key element for transmedia projects as it contributes to a sense of plausibility of the universes; multiplicity implies letting fans take advantage of different ways of telling stories, from different perspectives.

An example of continuity and multiplicity is the Kardashian-Jenner 2017 Christmas Card which was available on *E! Online* and then posted by Kourtney Kardashian on Instagram. The postcard shared a personal moment through a visual story, but at the same time, invited the audience to fill in a blank space, the absence of Kylie Jenner. In order to do so, fans could hear different family member's perspective on this matter, from a variety of media channels available (e.g., Instagram, TV Series, Twitter, online newspapers). The third binomial is immersion and extractability, being immersion achieved through the sensation of feeling part of the story and/or the chance to be part of the story world, and extractability related to the opportunities fans may have of 'taking' elements from the narrative universe (for instance, memorabilia or extra information). An example of immersion would be when Larsa Pippen starred in one of *KUWTK* episodes alongside Kourtney Kardashian in *E!*

Entertainment YouTube Channel, asking fans for their opinions and ideas for a new talk show. In terms of extractability, it can be argued that most business ventures founded by the family have become not only a way of pursuing the family's values and lifestyle, but also objects for merchandise, which followers are incorporating into their lives and routines. The fourth is worldbuilding, meaning the ability to create identifiable worlds. A depiction of this attribute is *KUWTK*'s plot itself. While performing a celebrity lifestyle, the family also performs an expressive panorama which humanizes these characters, making them more relatable. Seriality is the fifth principle, and it is based on the construction of a narrative that will be widespread in parts, which can be seen in the way different family members' lives have found a way into new forms of media, offering new content and perspectives. The sixth is subjectivity, in the sense that transmedia storytelling should allow individual interpretation, and encourage the sharing of experiences. *KUWTK* stands out since the audience is faced with real-life people, whose life stories are being shared on TV. The seventh, and last concept, is performance, in order to alert that the narrative structures must be able to articulate the creative performances of its fans. Considering that *KUWTK* is a reality TV series, performance plays an important part in withstanding the show's worldbuilding capacity. Additionally, it is possible to identify performance practices both by the Kardashians, as well as by their fans in other media, mainly in social media.

From Transmedia Storytelling to Transmedia Branding

The success of transmedia as an entertainment business model led to the implementation of its logics and narrative strategies into other areas, particularly branding. According to Tenderich (2013), transmedia branding is: "[…] a communication process in which information about a brand is packaged into an integrated narrative, which is dispersed in unique contributions across multiple media channels to create an interactive and engaging brand experience" (p. 3).

Tenderich (2013, 2014) considers that the design elements of a transmedia branding campaign are: narratives, participation and brands. Narratives are the stories to be told, taking advantage of different media; participation implies thinking about strategies to actively engage the audience; and brands are what consumers buy, it could be a product, a service, a company, or even an individual or a cause, and "[s]ome types of brands come naturally into a transmedia existence. These brands not only have a story, they *are* the story" (Tenderich, 2013: 8). This brand storytelling exists in the case of entertainment franchises like *Harry Potter* (Scolari, 2015), yet, the other brands can also present themselves as narrative worlds, as the case of Coca Cola and *The Happiness Factory*.

Likewise, Tenderich's three strategies can be applied to the case of the Kardashians. The transmedia unfolding of the Kardashians universe has been occurring in TV series and their spin offs, digital video content, books, mobile gaming, social media content, mobile device apps, perfumes, clothing, and beauty brands. These media work interdependently, each converging and adding new information about the story world. Thus, their narratives usually combine a multitude of product and celebrity branding strategies. This transmedia branding works cohesively towards an expansion of each family member's celebritization by the fans, without which the products would be unlikely as well known as they are today.

Personal Branding and Transmedia Celebrities

Celebrities and micro-celebrities are developing their fame through a variety of endorsements. This fame is due not exclusively to their importance to audiences, but also, as Choi and Berger (2009) argue, to the Internet. They have become global and, like their audiences, these entrepreneurs invest their resources into voicing political and social affairs and consequently influencing their fans (Choi & Berger, 2009, p. 314). Due to their ability to capture different audiences, one could argue that celebrities are increasingly playing an important role in influencing social opinion, and the use of transmedia storytelling strategies can be key for consolidating these roles.

Taking this into consideration, we consider that it is already possible to witness the extension of transmedia strategies to celebrity culture. Therefore, we would like to propose that a transmedia celebrity may be defined as a celebrity that takes advantage of transmedia storytelling principles, in order to assert herself not only as a celebrity but also as a brand. This branding means that one may consider that transmedia celebrity is a hybrid concept, implying not only narrative strategies to consolidate one's position as (super)star, but also as a brand, meaning that a transmedia celebrity may also be understood as an emerging business model. Despite being real people, transmedia celebrities present themselves as a fictional storyworld, which is the basis for telling different, but complementary stories, spread in several media, and targeting an interactive audience. Throughout the process of audience engagement, transmedia celebrities consolidate themselves also as a brand. Then the expansion of transmedia into celebrity culture is implying the articulation of transmedia storytelling, (personal) branding and celebrity logic.

Concerning the relationship that has been set between the Kardashians, and ethics, social media have been the main channels used. Kim Kardashian West was first addressed for her ethical behavior in the end of 2017 when PETA director Pamela Anderson made a plead directed to her against the use of fur, then on May 12th, she announced that she would be wearing exclusively faux-fur, a statement that was further discussed by several magazines and fans. Although not as publicly discussed, the KKW beauty products are cruelty-free, aligning the brand with sustainability issues.

Conclusion

The present chapter proposed the extension of transmedia storytelling into celebrity studies as a personal branding strategy to better engage with fans. This implies new ways to tell stories and, at the same time, new ways of promotion, by activating the celebrity as a brand, similarly to the case of the Kardashian family, which has been expanding their universe through transmedia strategies, asserting and activating themselves as brands in different dimensions. Nonetheless, the Kardashians, as other celebrities and micro-celebrities, have unarguably become opinion leaders. The recent eco-friendly turn may be a sign that they will be paying more attention to the spread of more ethical messages, which might have an impact on their fans' behavior. We hence want to assert that transmedia celebrities strategies may perform an important role in the consolidation of these new narratives, since they are based on storytelling and imply a closer relationship with the audience, offering fans the opportunity to be part of the story world.

References

Bruns, A. (2008). *Blogs, Wikipedia, Second Life and beyond*. New York: Peter Lang.

Choi, C. J. & Berger, R. (2009). Ethics of celebrities and their increasing influence in 21st century society. *Journal of Business Ethics*, 91, pp. 313-318.

Giovagnoli, M. (2011). *Transmedia storytelling*. s.l.: ETC Press.

Jenkins, H. (2003). Transmedia storytelling. *MIT Technology Review*. Retrieved from http://www.technologyreview.com/news/401760/transmedia-storytelling/.

Jenkins, H. (2006). *Convergence culture*. New York: New York University Press.

Jenkins, H. (2009). *The revenge of the origami unicorn*. Retrieved from http://henryjenkins.org/2009/12/the_revenge_of_the_origami_uni.html

Khamis, S., Ang, L. & Welling, R. (2017). Self-branding, 'micro-celebrity' and the rise of social media influencers. *Celebrity Studies*, 8 (2), pp. 191-208.

Kinder, M. (1991). *Playing with power in movies, television, and video games*. Berkeley: University of California Press.

Leavenworth, M.L. (2011).Transmedial texts and serialized narratives. *Transformative Works and Cultures*, 8. Retrieved from http://journal.transformativeworks.org/index.php/twc/article/view/361

Marwick, A. (2015). You may know me from Youtube (pp. 333-348). In Marshall, P. D. & Redmond, S. (Ed.). *A companion to celebrity*. Hoboken: John Wiley & Sons.

Marwick, A.,and Boyd, D. (2011). I Tweet Honestly, I Tweet Passionately. *New Media & Society*, 13, pp. 114–133.

Oppenheimer, J. (2017). *The Kardashians*. U.S.: St. Martin's Press.

Scolari, C.A. (2015). Transmedia storytelling. In Rossolatos, G. (Ed.). *Handbook of brand semiotics* (pp. 151-169). Kassel: Kassel University Press.

Senft, T. M. (2012). Microcelebrity and the branded self. In Hartley, J., Burgess, J. & Bruns, A. (Ed.). *A companion to new media dynamics* (pp. 346-354). West Sussex: Wiley-Blackwell.

Tenderich, B. (2013). *Design elements of transmedia branding*. Retrieved from archive.annenberglab.com.

Tenderich, B. (2014). *Transmedia branding*. Frankfurt: European Institute for Media Optimization.

Not That Glam: Marketing in DIY Fashion and #TFWGucci Meme Campaign

Vehbi Gorgulu

Abstract. The primary objective of the current chapter is to explore how brand managers employ Internet memes as a marketing tool. The current study focuses on #TFWGucci, which is marked for being one of the first structured collaborative memetic marketing campaigns in the world. By embracing a qualitative approach, the study will explore production and meaning-making processes of #TFWGucci campaign to understand how the celebrity culture in the traditional sense is being transformed with the current digital content creation and marketing practices.

Keywords: Internet meme, luxury brand, digital culture, memetic marketing, #TFWGucci.

Introduction

Ads are an important part of global popular culture, which are marked for being useful tools to market products and services via effective strategies and channels. Throughout the last decade, the ad industry has gone through a radical transformation. While commercial television, radio, and print ads were recognized for their strictly professional and structured production processes and the use of well-known figures such as celebrities, the Internet and its services have challenged these patterns. Especially since the Web 2.0 era, characterized by increased user interactivity and interaction, productions of user-generated content have transformed the traditional audience-producer relationship, as it has encouraged audiences to emerge as potential producers. Thus, user-generated, do-it-yourself (DIY) content production trends on the Internet have transformed traditional professional patterns for broadcasters.

This transformation has also had an impact on ads. For instance, the amateur fashion of user generated productions enabled everyday individuals to emerge as celebrities of the Internet era. While the Internet enabled emergence of its own celebrities, celebrities in the traditional sense have been the target of online humorous content producers. Memes, which are curated in an amateur, DIY fashion and offer humorous content, have become immensely popular among social media users. Meme accounts on Instagram such as @thefatjewish and @thebraintickle have millions of followers and have the power to reach individuals around the world in seconds. While mostly mocking current popular culture events in their agenda, meme creators also make fun of celebrities by inferring new meanings from their photographs, movie scenes, music and even professionally curated interviews.

As a low-budget but potentially an impactful practice, memes have also been on the radar of marketers. Many digital marketing agencies started to integrate Internet memes into the digital campaigns of their customers. Interestingly, one of these brands has been an Italian luxury brand of fashion and leather goods, Gucci, which is marked for offering luxurious and niche products to their consumers with a high fashion taste. With its Internet meme campaign, titled #TFGWGucci, Gucci hired various Internet meme producers to curate content for their marketing project that focused on promoting the brand's 2017 fashion line.

The current study explores Internet memes and marketing in DIY fashion, with a special focus on Gucci's #TFWGucci meme campaign, to discuss how Internet memes evolve conventional marketing strategies and have the potential to transform the existing popular culture.

Internet Meme as a Rising Phenomenon

The word 'meme' is originally an anthropological term coined by biologist Richard Dawkins (2016) in his famous "The Selfish Gene" book. While memes refer to the situation of "going viral" within a biological system within Dawkins' point of view, further studies interpreted the concept from a social perspective, especially within the context of products that go viral. Within this approach, memes can be defined as ideas, behaviors or styles that spread from one subject (person) to another within a culture (McCrae, 2017).

With the rise and widespread use of the Internet and social media, individuals wake up to various viral content called Internet memes. Internet memes are defined as jokes and/or ironic contexts in the form of video clips or photos, accompanied by textual captions (Shifman, 2011). They spread virally across the web if they are appealing to a large group of social media users. Internet memes are especially common in visual-based online social networks such as Instagram. For some, such as McCrae (2017), Internet memes are "redefining the communal experience, especially among millennials" in the age of "fragmented media and personalized algorithms".

Previous literature explores Internet memes as a tool of cultural reproduction in the case of #icebucketchallenge, which was a social media campaign to draw attention to ALS disorder that became popular in 2014 (Rossolatos, 2015). Similarly, Marcus and Singer (2017) analyze Internet memes that portray the Ebola outbreak of 2014-2015 from an ethnographic perspective and argue that such practices have great implications for social awareness of such crisis events. Decook's (2018) work indicates how internet memes can be used as a tool of propaganda. In their analysis, the alt-right affiliate movement the 'Proud Boys,' for example, is being promoted to mainly young American and Canadian men as a fraternity-like organization that celebrates 'Western ideals'.

In another study, Shifman (2011) argues Internet memes allow Internet users to create new meaning out of existing textual and visual materials. Additionally, Wigging and Bowers (2015) explain Internet memes encourage participation among members of the digital sphere and recognize meme production activity within the online remix culture. In another study, Shifman (2014) conceptualizes Internet memes as operative signs, which are designed as invitations for creative action.

Shifman (2015) also argues that memes are marked for sharing common characteristics, content form, and stance, which are circulated, imitated and transformed via the Internet by ordinary users of the Internet. One of the primary instances of Internet memes can be found in the re-adaptation of the "Keep Calm and Carry On" poster, which was first published by the Ministry of Information in Great Britain in 1993 (Felixmüller, 2017). Various versions of the "Keep Calm and Carry On" poster became an important element of the user-produced contents of the Internet-sphere, especially at the beginning of 2010s (for a re-interpretation, see Figure 1).

Fig. 1. An interpretation of the original "Keep Calm and Carry On" as an Internet meme. *Source:* knowyourmeme.com, 2018

Some of the most recent and popular examples of Internet memes can be found in viral contents that target the killing of Harambe, a gorilla who grabbed a three year old boy that climbed into a gorilla enclosure at the Cincinnati Zoo and Botanical Garden, and Nusret, a Turkish butcher-restaurant owner that became viral with his unique meat serving methods, Godfather-like image and fancy lifestyle. Especially the killing of Harambe drew worldwide attention for animal violence, which resulted in the emergence of thousands of memes on the Internet that mocked the controversial killing (for example, see Figure 2).

Fig 2. An Internet meme that narrates the killing of Harambe.

Internet memes are not only about portraying funny moments or criticism but also about creating and spreading trends. The Harlem Shake of 2013, in which a group of people danced to a short excerpt from the song, was an outstanding example of this, which encouraged viewers to imitate the dance routines in the original sample. In a short period of time, this dance routine turned into a global online trend. A more recent case has been with the Green Frog that portrayed an alien-like green frog dancing to El Chombo's "Dame tu Cosita" and it immediately became viral and imitated by millions. Similarly, another trend called the "Kiki Challenge" has come into prominence in 2018, after

Drake, a Canadian rapper, released the single "In My Feelings". For the Kiki Challenge, various individuals filmed themselves while jumping out of a moving vehicle and dancing on the road.

The aforementioned examples justify Jenkins' (2008) "participatory culture" argument, in which he claims that consumers turn into producers by creating and spreading new content. He also argues that participatory culture is a culture with low barriers to artistic expression, which remains relevant when considering the production processes on the Internet. This consideration is not solely limited to Internet memes but is also applicable in the context of video productions for YouTube and content creations for blogging services, where consumers emerge as potential producers and curate their own audiences. Such transformation in the traditional audience-producer relationship has also impacted the fashion industry, in which companies started looking for new ways to catch up with the rising online trends in order to appeal to their existing and potential consumers.

How are Memes Related to the Fashion Industry?

With the rise of Instagram culture, the integration of the fashion industry into online social networks has become inevitable since the beginning of the 2010s. Besides their existing online web sites, where they exhibited their new collections and made sales, various brands launched their own official Instagram accounts in order to reach larger audiences. Moreover, various Instagram users, who launched their own profiles to post their favorite fashion looks, also support these brands indirectly. Even in certain cases, brands adopted the trends their followers created, which has recently been the case with Gucci.

In March 2017, Gucci enacted an Instagram ad series that re-interpreted popular Internet memes by also featuring their new watch collection (Digital Gucci, 2017). In Alessandro Michele's words—who was the creative director of the project—the campaign intended to create a "desire to engage with a wider community than that which traditionally locates around the world of fashion" (Thompson, 2017). In line, the fashion house contacted meme creators such as @williamcult and @beigecardigan, who still curate captions for the visuals that "brings them to life as digital artifacts" (Gucci, 2017).

The memes of the campaign imitated the dialogue patterns of the creators. The Gucci collection products were associated with everyday social interactions in a mocking manner, which compose the majority of the contents curated by meme creators. Such social interactions include a son's unification with his family over Thanksgiving dinner, weird social situations such as the ones where someone misses a question during a social interaction and does not know what to say, or has no clue to answer the question so, rather reacts in a weird way (an example can be found at an Internet meme created by William Cult for the Gucci campaign[1]).

In a similar approach, Gucci and its collaborators mocked daily social interactions by associating the content with the brand's watch collection. For instance, in his contribution, Benjamin Langford (@blangblang92) associates the Gucci watch with a social situation where one's girlfriend does not recognize a style change on his outlook with faded flowers[2].

The campaign interestingly resulted in controversy, as various Internet users criticized the brand for advertising in an amateur-seeming fashion, while others praised the campaign for its originality. While some Instagram users supported the campaign by commenting, "They hate you for doing you but that's you, keep'em comin' babe" and "LMAO", others expressed their dislike with the campaign, by noting, "stop these series!?" and "I'm sorry as a consumer that can actually purchase your goods this does NOT work for me. It's silly and almost clown like" (instagram.com, 2018).

Within the first month of the campaign, Gucci reached 120 million people, approximately 2 million likes, 22,000 comments, and 0.5% engagement rate with its 30 memes (Hudson, 2017). Although 0.5% engagement rate can be interpreted as low for an average Internet campaign, it is higher than the Gucci's total average engagement rate, which is 0.41%. Moreover, two out of 30 Gucci memes provided the brand with the highest engagement rate among its whole Instagram posts with 1.55% (Hudson, 2017). So results can be perceived as a success in the context of Gucci's history with online ads.

Although some perceived the Gucci meme campaign as a strategic failure, the experience should rather be interpreted as an instance of interplay with advances in communication technologies, as brands aim to make the most of these technological opportunities. This experience also shows us how "glam" in the traditional sense is open to experimentation and evolution with advancements in new technologies.

One should also recognize Jenkins (2008) in recognizing #TFWGucci campaign as a typical part of what he calls participatory culture. Here, consumers (meme creators) emerge as leading actors in the creation of a campaign project for a luxury fashion brand, by curating narratives and designing visuals in line with the format of a particular social network. The

---

[1] Cult's work can be found here: http://digital.gucci.com/tfwgucci/p/23

[2] Langford's work can be found here: http://digital.gucci.com/tfwgucci/p/23

Gucci example differentiates itself from the former customized design competition attempts of brands such as Pepsi and GAP, where contestants had limited power to say and works of competitors were evaluated by juries.

Although online social networks may seem like an appealing tool for many brands, they should create and curate unique strategies that work the best for them. Gucci's DIY-seeming meme campaign was a good example of this situation. The campaign aimed to attract attention among wider audiences and it succeeded when compared with the brand's previous online marketing attempts.

Discussion: Ethical Glamour and Beyond Fashion Marketing

This emerging organic, DIY culture that is mainly represented by Internet memes on social media can be read as a power shift between producers and users. When traditional media platforms dominated pop culture, a cultural imposition was taking place in which users played a limited role as interpreters/consumers. However, on social media, users collectively have the power to promote trends that they favor. This does not have to be necessarily in the form of collaborating with brands. Some of these trends can even be perceived as activists and system opponents.

One of these trends is the "no makeup culture" that remains essential for promoting healthy body image, especially for younger generations. So far, more than 16 million photos are shared on Instagram with the hashtag #nomakeup, and this trend inevitably impacted on the mainstream pop culture, as celebrities like Alicia Keys explained they will not be using makeup anymore. Thus, in terms of creating social change, one has to look at the positive examples of using social media that promote healthy body images and even eating and exercising habits. By supporting this argument, one should not underestimate the power of role models such as Kim Kardashian and Kylie Jenner that are famous for their looks promoting perfection in their own ways. The point is, rather than imitating these role models that continue the already established norms of glam culture, ordinary Internet users can find and create their own socially sensitive and natural interpretations of fashion.

It can be stated here that Gucci is one of the very first brands to recognize the potential and power of users on social media; by reversing the traditional producer-audience relationship, they imitate what the average Internet user made popular. The #TFGWGucci campaign not only effectively employed Internet memes as a marketing strategy, but it also started a discussion for reconsideration of the ordinary and the luxurious.

While Internet memes are mostly recognized by their amateur design and basic content, luxurious brands mostly utilize from high-budget marketing strategies coming into existence on billboards, TV, and even niche media. Despite intense criticism, the campaign claimed that even brands such as Gucci, which are associated with high taste and fashion, must be integrated with the Internet technologies and cultures to sustain their longevity and connect with their audiences. The campaign revealed how new tools, actors, and strategies challenged the popular culture. Thus, it has also inevitably encouraged researchers to reconsider established concepts associated with pop culture, such as glam and luxury.

As the final word, it can be noted that Internet memes are not at their best, in terms of fostering healthy body images, eating or exercising habits. In currently mainstream memes, social values like apathy, lethargy, and hypocrisy are being promoted by mocking daily interactions of individuals among their families or workplaces. Ageism, sexism and promotion of bad consumption habits are still encouraged, albeit in a humorous manner.

Still, it should be recalled that similar to what Gucci did to promote its 2017 watch collection, slow fashion movement supporters that are pushing back against the pressure to deliver new products at an ever-faster clip can work for challenging the existing mock culture on Internet memes, by integrating socially and environmentally informative messages on sensitive issues through mockery. Slow fashion, which is already a considerable trend in Instagram with #slowfashion, #slowfashionmovement and #slowfashionblogger with more than 2 million posts, can turn into a global trend that is not only supported by a minor segment of Internet users, but also by average fashion consumers that are not aware of the existing impositions.

In that sense, social media and visual-based avenues like Instagram are not only useful to challenge the dominant marketing strategies but also to discover and create new trends that have the potential to transform existing norms and perceptions of the mainstream fashion world. Memes are one of the most essential, low-budget and impactful tools to foster this transformation. The process has begun; it only needs further pushes of celebrities, social brands and sensitive DIY social media producers.

References

Dawkins, R. (2016). *The selfish gene: 40th anniversary edition.* Oxford University Press.

Decook, J.R. (2018). Memes and symbolic violence: #proudboys and the use of memes for propaganda and the construction of collective identity. *Learning Media and Technology*, 43(4), 485-504, doi: 10.1080/17439884.2018.1544149

Digital Gucci. (2017). #TFWGucci artworks, available at http://digital.gucci.com/tfwgucci/p/1 (Accessed 12 July 2018)

Felixmüller, M.L. (2017). Warburg's cultural psychology as a tool for understanding Internet memes. *Philosophy of Photography,* 8(1&2), 211-220.

Gucci. (2017). Gucci official website, available at http://www.gucci.com (Accessed 24 July 2018).

Hudson, D. (2017). Gucci gone meme: The luxury house throws us a curveball. March 22, 2017, available at https://blog.dashhudson.com/gucci-meme-luxury-brand-instagram marketing-content-strategy/ (Accessed 12 June 2018)

Instagram (2018). http://www.instagram.com (Accessed 11 May 2018)

Jenkins, H. (2008). *Convergence culture: Where old and new media collide.* NYU Press.

Marcus, O.R., & Singer, M. (2017). Loving Ebola-chan: Memes in an epidemic. *Media, Culture & Society,* 39(3), 341-356.

McCrae, J. (2017). Meme marketing: How brands are speaking a new consumer language. Forbes, May 8, 2017, available at https://www.forbes.com/sites/forbescommunicationscouncil/2017/05/08/mememarketing-how-brands-are-speaking-a-new-consumer-language/#6c82843e37f5 (Accessed 13 March 2018)

Rossolatos, G. (2015). The ice-bucket challenge: The legitimacy of the memetic mode of cultural reproduction. *Signs and Society,* 3(1), 132-152.

Shifman, L. (2011). An anatomy of a YouTube meme. *New Media & Society*, 14(2), 187-203.

Shifman, L. (2014). The cultural logic of photo-based meme genres. *Journal of Visual Culture,* 13(3), 340-358.

Shifman, L. (2015). Memeology Festival 05. Memes as ritual, virals as transmission? In praise of blurry boundaries – Culture Digitally', available at, http://culturedigitally.org/2015/11/memeology-festival-05-memes-as-ritual-viralsastransmission-in-praise-of-blurry-boundaries/. (Accessed 10 Dec. 2018)

Thompson, R. (2017). Gucci posted a load of weird memes and the Internet is cringing hard. *Mashable*, March 21, 2017, available at https://mashable.com/2017/03/21/guccimeme-ad-campaign/#TtZkfk_UGgqM (Accessed 13 April 2018)

Wiggins, B.E., & Bowers, G.B. (2015). Memes as genre: A structurational analysis of the memescape. *New Media & Society,* 17(11), 1886-1906.

Estonian Fashion/Beauty Bloggers' Practices and Ethical Dilemmas in Featuring Branded and Sponsored Content

Maria Murumaa-Mengel and Piia Õunpuu

Abstract. The aim of this study is to explore the practices and perceived ethical dilemmas of beauty and fashion bloggers when featuring sponsored posts on their blogs. Based on qualitative in-depth interviews (n=10) conducted with popular Estonian bloggers and expert interviews with representatives of the Estonian Consumer Protection Board (ECPB), we can notice confusion and emergence of vague self-regulating principles when discussing branded or sponsored content. The ECPB has acknowledged social media influencers as agents that increasingly need attention and regulation. However, they admit lacking the know-how and resources to develop and enforce any formal regulations. Interviewed bloggers seem to be fairly aware of regulations in other countries, but at the same time, they are quite selective and ambiguous in following these in their own content production practices. There seems to be a general shift of responsibility - decoding sponsored posts as such is often perceived as audience's duty and competence.

Keywords: ethics, influencer marketing, beauty bloggers, #ad, sponsored content.

Introduction

More and more people turn to online influencers for inspiration and recommendations for their purchases or other decisions. Bloggers, YouTubers, Instagram celebrities—the contemporary influencers and microcelebrities—are trusted by their audiences because they often appear to be essentially regular people, who are producing "highly engaging and personalized content" (Abidin, 2018: 71). We acknowledge the fact that using the term "blogger" in the title and description of this study does not fully describe the multi-platform content production these influencers engage in, as they are often taking meticulous care of their "cross-platform digital estates" (Abidin, 2017), but for clarity we chose a term that described their dominant platform. In parallel with "bloggers" we will also use the term "influencer", defined by Abidin (2018) as professional career-focused multimedia microcelebrities for whom microcelebrity is not merely a hobby, but also increasingly career and profit-oriented.

These online-celebrities invite the audiences to be a part of their everyday life, present different aspects of their personal and professional sphere and continuously produce and perform the kind of authenticity that invites para-social identification (Arvidsson et al., 2015). At the same time, these online influencers often monetize their authenticity-based following and popularity by producing sponsored or branded content—which can provide a substantial income—turning them into modern creative entrepreneurs, who, in addition to keeping up an appearance, need to keep in mind their revenue streams directly connected to that branded self (Duffy & Hund, 2015; Nathanson, 2014). When focusing on these "commercial bloggers'" (Abidin, 2018: 74) content about beauty and fashion, we can mostly notice sponsored posts (#ad, #sponsored, etc.) endorsing and promoting clothing lines, make-up brands or travel service providers. Usually, questions about ethics of social media influencers and their content are sparked when we see paid collaborations that involve alcohol, quick cash loans, online casinos, dietary supplements or smoking/vaping. Two typical sub-discussions are about the possibility of regulation in these online spaces and/or the contemporary digital literacies (Buckingham, 2007; Rheingold, 2010) of online audiences.

We were intrigued by these initial observations and set out to explore and understand how aware are the influencers of their own marketing and disclosing practices, especially when these #ad messages are made to look as organic as possible. More specifically, we ask how do Estonian beauty/fashion bloggers disclose sponsored/branded content? Secondly, what are the bloggers' typical perceived ethical dilemmas in featuring sponsored posts?

Background

The core and power of influencer marketing lie in the influencers' role as word-of-mouth (WoM) agents, a well-established theory by Katz and Lazarsfeld (1955). Obviously, in previous times WoM meant something completely different and, today, we can speak about e-WoM agents who have taken the role of opinion leaders into online spaces and online audiences. Many influencers have gathered massive online followings that are interested in their day-to-day life, but also trust opinions and recommendations made about certain products or services. Influencers usually present themselves as authentic and available, using social media that allows direct communication with followers and adding to the perceived authenticity (Senft, 2010). Subsequently, the marketing messages they convey have been found to be more effective compared to traditional advertising (de Vries, Gensler & Leeflang, 2012).

In many countries, where social media influencers earn an income monetizing their online presence and authorities have acknowledged their role as marketing agents, relevant and clear guidelines have been developed. Some examples include the Advertising Standards Authority guidelines for social media conduct in the United Kingdom (An Influencer's…, 2018), the Consumer Ombudsman regulations (The Consumer…, 2018) in Norway or the Federal Trade Commission guidelines (The FTC's…, 2017) in the United States. The latter has also called out highly popular social media influencers on misconduct (Dalton, 2017). Also, bottom-up self-regulating frameworks have been established, for example, in Finland, where a guideline for ethical blogging (Eettinen…, 2018) has been developed.

Estonian bloggers have no such guidelines to follow. The main regulatory document is the Estonian Advertising Act, which sets general rules for all advertorial content. However, as the Advertising Act is fairly outdated, focuses on traditional media and is generally vague in its wording, it is not seen as a credible and trustworthy source for social media content.

Overall, the Estonian blogging community is a fairly sizeable one, taking into account the small population of 1.3 million people. There is no systematic overview of the field, but we can gain some insight from available fragmented statistics, for example, an online catalogue eestiblogid.ee trying to map Estonian blogs has listed 152 blogs in the beauty and fashion category. An annual awards ceremony dedicated to bloggers has had an average of 277 participating blogs each year, dominated by fashion and lifestyle bloggers. Estonian communication agency JLP has mapped 700 notable microcelebrities and influencers in a recent study, 66% of whom had been contacted by a brand for collaboration (Blogibaromeeter…, 2018). Obviously, it is a highly dynamic field, with people leaving and entering the system constantly, engaging in and renouncing "aspirational labor" (Duffy & Hund, 2015) that goes into achieving and maintaining influence.

As is the case elsewhere, most (fashion and beauty) bloggers are female. Recently we have seen the rise of occasional notable male influencers active on Instagram, however, at the time of conducting this study, they did not have a significant following.

Most local beauty and fashion bloggers produce content in Estonian, but there is a growing number of English or Estonian+English blogs. As the size of the Estonian market and the audience is limited, especially when compared to international influencers, using English can be a means to be approachable to a larger audience. The brands working with Estonian bloggers are both local brands, such as natural cosmetics brands, hotels or food brands. International brands with a local market in Estonia are present as well (such as clothing brands).

Estonian context of sponsored collaborations provides some notable cases where ethics in (commercial) blogging have been in focus: one alcohol brand invited fashion bloggers to a glamorous photoshoot in a hotel, resulting in branded Instagram and blog posts, highlighting the desirable lifestyle associated with expensive alcohol. Another example involves bloggers who collaborated with an SMS-loan provider, suggesting that a quick cash loan was a great way to fund their activities and purchases. Multiple bloggers have recommended a brand of weight loss tea to their partly underage following.

We find this topic to have increasing importance, as (young) people's media repertoires are changing rapidly and traditional media, dominated by public figures and mainstream celebrities, is increasingly overshadowed by young social media and internet celebrities (Abidin, 2018). The rules and norms are ever-evolving and many online spaces and practices can be considered to be a part of unregulated "jungle".

Methods and Data

For this study, we conducted semi-structured interviews with ten popular bloggers in Estonia, who can all be categorized as fashion and/or beauty bloggers. We considered it important to narrow the field of the influencers down to a specific one, as principles of collaborating with brands or marketing opportunities can vary in fitness-, mommy-, food- or tech-bloggers' content. We determined the popularity of the bloggers by tracking the social media following of different prominent bloggers on different platforms (blogs, Instagram, Facebook), as well as visibility in marketing campaigns and local social media awards winners' lists.

Participants of this study were all Estonian, female, between the ages of 17 and 31, and blogging for six years in average. Quotes from the interviews in the Results are marked as, for example, B(blogger)1(order of conducted interviews)_22(age)_5(years in blogging). Most of the participants used their blog as a dominant platform, but used Facebook and Instagram simultaneously as supporting platforms.

Three main categories were deductively constructed for the interview plan – everyday practices of bloggers, attitudes towards different forms of collaborations, and discussions about ethics. The interviews were analyzed using within-case and cross-case qualitative thematic text analysis (Braun & Clarke, 2006), combining inductive analytical logic and codes with previously established main categories.

To get a broader view, context and understanding of this topic, we conducted semi-structured expert interviews with the representatives of the Estonian Consumer Protection Board to grasp the official level of regulation regarding social media influencers and discussions taking place on the institutional level.

Results and Discussion

Interviewed bloggers seem to be fairly aware of regulations on disclosing branded content in other countries. However, they are quite selective and ambiguous in following these practices in their own blogs. As our findings show, sponsored posts can be (intentionally) completely inseparable from organic content. We suggest that the bloggers feel an obligation towards their audience to be honest, independent and trustworthy. In other words, self-presentation practices are based on the notion of authentic self (Marwick, 2015) and revealing commercial interests can shatter this perception for their audiences. So we see an expectation that sponsored posts are something shameful, being a "sell-out" in a sense. Thus, notifications of commercial collaborations are often marked in smaller text at the end of the post, or encoded by the bloggers as advertorials by using hyperlinks and text in bold, relying on the audience members' ability to decode these messages correctly:

B3_19_3: *Basically, when I write the introduction, then I still, I mean, if you read through it, it should kind of indicate that the product was sent to me.*

When the branded nature of a post is disclosed, it is often with the English #sponsored, not the Estonian equivalent.

Furthermore, the bloggers constructed their followers mostly to be "ideal audiences" (Marwick & boyd, 2011; boyd, 2014; Murumaa-Mengel, 2017) – perfect recipients of their messages and information who share similar values, knowledge and have the right interpretative lens to decode the messages. So our participants imagined their audiences to be dedicated readers who are able to recognize influencers' collaboration partners.

B7_31_10: *It's enough when the brand is tagged /.../ the followers will understand themselves if it's sponsored or not sponsored. /.../ When a person is mature enough, they will understand very well that models get paid, designers get paid. /.../ And if you follow someone, for whom blogging is a job, then their whole content is sponsored anyway.*

Of course, in reality, bloggers' audiences are far more multifaceted, consisting of long-time followers, fans, lurkers, occasional readers, random "stumblers" or even anti-fans.

At the time of these interviews, there were only two bloggers who had a clear system for indicating sponsored or collaborative posts on their blogs. Other interviewees used inconsistent and often haphazard strategies to mark such posts, e.g. with a brief sentence in the introduction of the post, such as "I was sent" or "I had the opportunity to review", if anything:

B1_28_5: *I say it in the text that I had a chance to do something with [a clothing brand]. To me the word "chance" already means that I didn't go to the store and buy three of their outfits.*

When we asked about perceived ethical dilemmas in connection to specific goods or services, many interviewed bloggers highlighted the importance to stay authentic and true to their own brand and personal values. Many of them ruled out any possible collaborations with brands that sell furs or do not follow animal rights in their production practices. Non-smokers and non-drinkers noted that they would never feature alcohol or cigarette brands.

In Estonia, the regulatory institution keeping an eye on the advertising market is the Estonian Consumer Protection Board (ECPB). Interviewed experts from ECPB noted that so-called "advertorials" on social media, as a whole, are a fairly new topic for them, one with which they presently have neither the time nor the resources or knowledge to deal with. According to the Estonian Advertising Act, the advertorial nature (which also includes sponsored content) of any media should be understandable and noticeable to the consumer at their usual state of attention. Laws are stricter on financial services, tobacco, dietary supplements and alcohol, however on social media, the compliance to those laws is scarce, according to interviews conducted with the representatives of the ECPB.

As there have not yet been any high profile legal cases or thorough discussions in Estonia about paid ad spaces of influencers, nor any repercussions against misconduct, the bloggers seem to cross their fingers and hope for the best, even if they admit to struggling with the ground rules. Interestingly, interviewed bloggers voiced the need for clear official regulations – either from the ECPB, the Tax and Customs Board or by the Advertising Act, although that would probably decrease and limit their opportunities for publishing commercial content.

To understand why some posts are perceived as worthy of a sponsorship disclosure and others not, we asked the interviewed bloggers to define and give examples of sponsored social media posts. Usually, sponsorships and commercial collaborations are clearly understood as such when money is being exchanged, when there is a contract and clear, agreed on rules between the blogger and a brand (or mediating agencies). But a great deal of the bloggers' participation in marketing campaigns is based on gifting–"receiving freebies in exchange for shout-outs and mentions" (Abidin, 2018: 74) where no monetary compensation is involved. A number of the interviewed bloggers of our study did not define sharing gifts from brands as a sponsored post:

B6_22_7: *I mean, I know, that I don't have to post about these gifts. But often I still do, and especially when I like the product, for example, a brand really surprises me, then I still do, I don't know, an Instagram Story or something.*

The bloggers noted that they often link to the brand's profile with an @ symbol as a way to refer to the branded nature of the post. We can interpret such gifting practices as aspirational labor (Duffy & Hund, 2015), an effort to broaden the bloggers' opportunities and invite brands into collaboration by making the first move and giving more to the brand that could be expected.

Conclusions

Fashion and beauty bloggers of our study admit struggling to navigate the authentic-commercial content or straightforward-encoded communication. Ethical issues surface for bloggers when confronted with products or services that are in conflict with personal values and beliefs (e.g., alcohol, furs, etc.), but issues of clear distinction of commercial messages and disclosure of economic gain as e-WoM agents are rarely thought through. While posts for which monetary compensation is received, are easier to define and potentially disclosed with a sentence in the beginning or end of the post, a large number of branded collaborations on Estonian influencers' social media are based on gifting, where it is much more difficult to draw the line between kindness in sharing a nice product and #sponsored advertorials.

As the field of social media and influencer marketing lacks (self)regulation in Estonia, the ECPB, is in turn troubled by the lack of institutional basis that could be held accountable for any misconduct. From a consumer's perspective, the ECPB's biggest concern is marketing campaigns featuring influencers that promote alcohol, dietary supplements, different gambling or financial services. Influencer marketing remains a fairly unregulated grey area in Estonia, needing to catch up with countries where the field is more developed and modifying existing frameworks for the local context.

On a more abstract level, bloggers still seem to distinguish online and offline as separate and actions in one sphere not overlapping with the other. Internet researchers have long moved on from the position of opposed real and virtual spheres and identities (e.g., Turkle, 1995), to contextualizing the online world and online-self as not the opposite of real, separated and independently existing but as intertwined, affecting each other, making up an augmented reality

(Jurgenson, 2012) and augmented self. This change is not necessarily accepted and internalized by the general public and within that public, the fashion and beauty bloggers who imagine themselves to be communicating with "ideal" audiences and, without clear rules or responsibility.

Another broad aspect is in relation to audiences' agency – we notice a shift of responsibility where decoding sponsored posts as such is often perceived as audience's duty and competence and thus a matter of media or digital literacies. Although self-directed learning and peer-to-peer knowledge-sharing is important, other various stakeholders are expected to make a contribution. We suggest a regular revision of media/information/digital literacies frameworks and policies to include influential agents and practices of social media.

References

Abidin, C. (2017). Influencer Extravaganza: Commercial "Lifestyle" Microcelebrities in Singapore. In: *The Routledge Companion to Digital Ethnography* (pp. 184-194). Routledge.

Abidin, C. (2018). *Internet Celebrity: Understanding Fame Online*. UK: Emerald Publishing.

Arvidsson, A., Caliandro A., Airoldi M. & Barina S. (2015). Crowds and value. Italian directioners on Twitter. *Information, Communication & Society. 19*. DOI: 10.1080/1369118X.2015.1064462

An Influencer's Guide to making clear that ads are ads (2018, October 3). Advertising Standards Authority. Retrieved from https://www.asa.org.uk/uploads/assets/uploaded/3af39c72-76e1-4a59-b2b47e81a034cd1d.pdf

Blogibaromeeter 2018. (2018). *JLP web page*. Retrieved from http://www.jlp.ee/blogibaromeeter-2018/

Boyd, D. M. (2014). *It's complicated: The social lives of networked teens*. New Haven: Yale University.

Braun, V., & Clarke, V. (2006). Using thematic analysis in psychology. *Qualitative research in psychology, 3*(2).

Buckingham, D. (2007). Media education goes digital: an introduction. *Learning, Media and Technology, 32*(2), 111-119. doi: 10.1080/17439880701343006

Dalton, M. (2017). Social-Media Stars Are Turning Heads—of Regulators. *The Wall Street Journal*. Retrieved from https://www.wsj.com/articles/social-media-influencers-get-noticed-by-regulators-1513342801 de Vries, L., S. Gensler & P.S.H. Leeflang. (2012). Popularity of brand posts on brand fan pages: An investigation of the effects of social media marketing. *Journal of Interactive Marketing* 26(2). doi:10.1016/j.intmar.2012.01.003

Duffy, B. E., & Hund, E. (2015). "Having it All" on Social Media: Entrepreneurial Femininity and Self-Branding Among Fashion Bloggers. *Social Media + Society* 1(2). https://doi.org/10.1177/2056305115604337

Eettinen ohjeistus. (2018). Indiedays. Retrieved from http://www.indiedays.com/item/tietoja/eettinen-ohjeistus

Jurgenson, N. (2012). When atoms meet bits: Social media, the mobile web and augmented revolution. *Future Internet, 4*(1), 83-91

Katz, E. & Lazarsfeld, P. F. (1955). *Personal influence: The part played by people in the flow of mass communications.* New York: The Free Press.

Marwick, A. E. (2015). Instafame: Luxury selfies in the attention economy. *Public culture, 27*(1(75)), 137-160.

Marwick, A. E., & boyd, d. m. (2011). I tweet honestly, I tweet passionately: Twitter users, context collapse, and the imagined audience. *New Media & Society, 13*(1), 114-133.

Murumaa-Mengel, M. (2017). *Managing Imagined Audiences Online: Audience Awareness as a Part of Social Media Literacies.* Doctoral Dissertation, media and communication. Tartu: University of Tartu Press.

Rheingold, H. (2010). Attention, and Other 21st-Century Social Media Literacies. *EDUCAUSE Review*, 45(5), 14-16.

Senft, T. M. (2010). Microcelebrity and the Branded Self. In: A *Companion to New Media Dynamics*. Doi: 10.1002/9781118321607.ch22

The Consumer Authority's guidance on labelling advertising in social media (2018, October 3). Forbruker Ombudet. Retrieved from https://forbrukerombudet.no/english/guidelines/guidelines-labelling-advertisements-in-social-media

The FTC's Endorsement Guides: What People Are Asking. (2017). Federal Trade Commission. Retrieved from https://www.ftc.gov/tips-advice/business-center/guidance/ftcs-endorsement-guides-what-people-are-asking

Turkle, S. (1995). *Life on the screen. Identity in the age of the Internet.* New York: Touchstone.

Beauty Entrepreneur with Social Conscience: Rihanna Gets Real with her Power and Influence

Jaleesa Reed and Katalin Medvedev

Abstract. Global superstar Robyn "Rihanna" Fenty is no stranger to entrepreneurial endeavors. Since her first studio album in 2006, Rihanna has ventured into fashion, philanthropy, diplomacy, and beauty. This paper describes her ascension as a dominant player in the beauty industry as the creator and owner of the cosmetics line, Fenty Beauty. Rihanna's decision to intertwine her celebrity persona with Fenty Beauty has led to unprecedented success for products that advocate for visibility and voice for women of color in the beauty industry.

Keywords: beauty, Rihanna, Fenty Beauty, women of color, cosmetics.

Introduction

Music icon Robyn 'Rihanna' Fenty has earned a central place in popular culture. The spectrum of her talents is evident from the 156 music awards (nine of them Grammys) she has won since 2005 and her 2014 Council of Fashion Designers of America Fashion Icon Award. Rihanna has also been involved with the celebration and promotion of Black beauty through the creation of the Fenty Beauty makeup line. It is easy to see Rihanna's similarity with the first African American beauty entrepreneur Madam C. J. Walker. Like her predecessor, Rihanna is a self-made millionaire, Black beauty entrepreneur and advocate.

This paper uses Black feminist epistemology (Collins, 2002) as a framework to analyze Rihanna's lived experiences as the creator of Fenty Beauty for Makeup Art Cosmetics (MAC). Rihanna's interest in enhancing Black beauty dates back to intently watching her mother apply makeup. She was so fascinated by the process that she ended up as a child creating an early form of body lava, a moisturizer with shimmer. Over time, Rihanna learned about the value of appearance management as a tool of agency and fulfillment. She was also confronted with the reality of Black women who were at times driven to crying because they could not find a skin-matching foundation in mainstream makeup brands. Rihanna's recognition of her own imperfections, others' life experiences, family history and turbulent personal life make her relatable among her fans. Consumers show up to buy Fenty Beauty products in record numbers because Rihanna's fame indirectly validates Black women and their beauty needs.

The collective experiences of Black women have informed the beauty philosophy of Fenty Beauty:

> The first woman I saw put makeup on her face was a Black woman – my mom – and when I think of my customers, I want everyone to feel like they can find their color, that they are represented as part of this new generation. (Fenty Beauty, 2017)

Rihanna collaborated with MAC on three product lines before she launched her namesake, Fenty Beauty, in 2017. Fenty Beauty's success is intertwined with Rihanna's projection of herself as an epitome of millennial authenticity and a promoter of a socially-sensitive beauty agenda.

With Fenty, she drew on Black millennial women's fascination with luxury brands. She also capitalized on her cultural influence to showcase a need and a market for makeup that embraced *all* skin tones.

Makeup for Women of Color

MAC is known for the strong color pigments used in its quality cosmetics, which allow the products to blend well on a range of skin tones. On the surface, MAC appears to be a true ally of diversity, considering that their motto is "all ages, all sexes, and all races." The repeated use of *all* implies that every individual can benefit from the use of their products. While MAC provides 20+ foundation shades, so do other luxury cosmetic brands such as Bobbi Brown and NARS. What is different, however, is MAC's savvy use of Rihanna as a celebrity endorser to attract Black female consumers.

Consumers experience Rihanna's celebrity persona through consumption. Thus, Rihanna's identity as a Black Barbadian woman is filtered through her celebrity status to the consumer. McCracken (1989) describes this process as a transfer of meanings from the celebrity's cultural context to the consumer through the celebrity's product endorsement. While McCracken (1989) argues that the consumer is the final point in this meaning transfer, Banister and Cocker (2014) argue that consumers can now choose to interact with celebrities by using social media. Thus, the relationship between celebrities and fans is an ongoing, reciprocal interaction.

 Rihanna established trust with consumers by actually working in the lab to "mix different textures with different colors" and learn "about the detail of makeup and what makes [products] look different" (Conti and Naughton, 2013). She advocated for foundation formulas with more variation in green, blue, and pink undertones, in addition to yellow and red, which suggests her genuine understanding of skin tone differences. Women of color have, for years, lamented about the lack of cosmetics matching their skin color (Lowman, 2015). Along with white hegemonic beauty norms that ignore Black women's needs, this was partly due to companies misunderstanding skin colors.

Undertones are classified as cool, warm, or neutral. Cool tones imply that the base tone of the skin is pink, red, or blue. Yellow or gold is the base tone for warm tones, and a neutral undertone is a mixture of cool and warm. In the past, cosmetic companies simply added black or red dye to deepen the color of the original foundation formula made for white women (Lowman, 2015). However, this was not fully effective because it did not account for the subtle shifts in skin color undertones.

Like Fenty Beauty, Make Up Forever, a mid- to high-range priced makeup brand, also provides foundation for a range of skin tones. They advertise their products emphasizing their "40 shades for everyone's unique skin tone" and an "understanding of the difference between red and yellow undertones" (Morel, 2017). While Rihanna agreed, she called the Make Up Forever foundations "still ashy" in her comment on their Instagram post (Morel, 2017) – suggesting there was a need for her own brand's perspective on skin tone diversity. According to makeup artist Derek Selby, the skin accepts the undertone color which compliments it, and reflects the shade that does not (Lowman, 2015). With the wrong undertone and foundation, consumers can appear red or washed out and grey, regardless of the base color visible in the bottle. Thus, Rihanna's colloquial "still ashy" comment refers to the grey color left behind when using a foundation like Make Up Forever. To fully understand and recognize consumers of color, subtleties in their skin tone must be recognized and incorporated into products.

The Reality of Celebrities as "Best Friends"

In today's cosmetic marketplace, celebrity cosmetic brands, such as the Kylie Cosmetics Lip Kit by Kylie Jenner, signify a fan base tied to any celebrity's focus on their strategies for appearance management. The Kylie Cosmetics lip kits were born out of Jenner's lip insecurities and her desire to have fuller lips (Marine, 2018). Her personal backstory of this imperfection, which reveals that she is not flawless and is vulnerable, makes her relatable. By disclosing this in social media, the power differentials between celebrity and consumer appear to subside. Jenner's social media presence solidifies the trust between her and the lipkit user by openly sharing anecdotes such as her first kiss. It reveals how public comments about her lips left lasting impressions on her, causing her to seek lip filler injections (Schaefer, 2016). Jenner has identified the connection between the success of her lip kits and her insecurities, stating that "people could see that it's authentic to me, and it was organic, and it just worked" (Marine, 2018).

Newholm and Hopkinson (2009) argue that in capitalism, consumers develop understandings of their identity through consumption, and celebrities reinforce this process through brand and product association. If the consumer agrees with the celebrity, s/he also agrees with the cultural brands and symbols that are promoted by them. Some of today's celebrities want you to think of them as your "friend." While their status may seem unattainable, when they intentionally slip information about their insecurities and flaws, celebrities temporarily place themselves at the same social level as their fans. As 'friends,' celebrities convince consumers that their glamorous level of beauty is attainable, if they invest and use the same tools, time, and attention to product details.

Celebrities use Twitter and YouTube to reveal the "processes, pressures and negotiations" behind their social platform presence and the work that goes into developing their online persona (Thomas, 2014). On YouTube, Jenner and Rihanna have taken their audience to a new level of celebrity and fan interaction. They have compressed the labor-intensive work of a fully made-up face to a reasonable amount of time in Beauty Secrets on *Vogue's* YouTube channel. Rihanna (Vogue, 2018a) and Jenner (Vogue, 2018b) both recorded a 10-minute video showcasing their products and personality. Rihanna presented an "epic" guide to "going-out makeup" (Vogue, 2018a), while Jenner's video (Vogue, 2018b) is a guide to "lip, brows, and confidence." Each video demonstrates how these two celebrities construct their external appearance to match their personalities. The videos literally take the viewers to their bathrooms and allow a glimpse into how they create their perfect looks from start to finish. Sharing their beauty secrets and allowing their fans to follow along creates virtual intimacy between them and the audience- and trust for their brands.

While there are similarities in Jenner's and Rihanna's approaches—both leverage their experiences with society's beauty standards for profit—Rihanna's claim to authenticity differs from that of Jenner. Rihanna allows fans to recognize her vulnerability by disclosing private facts about her domestic abuse or humble beginnings. She presents appearance management to her fans as a soft power (Nye, 2004) tactic, suggesting that confidence and comfort with one's external presentation can translate into empowerment and help overcome hardship. From a personal standpoint, Rihanna understands skin tone diversity. She is also ready to share her knowledge to make sure her products are perfect for consumers. She uses her embodied knowledge to become the best marketing tool for her brand and communicate meanings and inspiration to the consumer (Carroll, 2009). The physical and affective labor she performs on behalf of her fans invests Fenty Beauty with an aura of authenticity. While Jenner's insecurities resonate with many people as well, her solutions to overcome them are more commercial; they depend primarily on beauty trends and one's financial means. Rihanna's beauty agenda goes further because it also hints at an agenda for social and racial justice.

Influencing the Model Type

In the first Fenty Beauty promotion, the camera races around a concrete city, capturing women clothed in fashionable fitness wear known as athleisure, with "perfect skin, not makeup skin" (Fenty Beauty by Rihanna, 2017). This look of natural perfection is the product of what Wissinger (2015) calls "glamour labor." Rihanna understands and commodifies glamour labor on multiple levels. By appearing relatable, she manages to mask the considerable energy and costs required to create her perfect skin and the fact that it is only possible because a huge team is working tirelessly behind the scenes to manage every detail of her flawless appearance.

The promotion of different types of beauty is apparent in the Fenty Beauty launch video, which features models like Slick Woods and Duckie Thot. In the fashion industry, Black models "bring a higher level of aesthetic skills" to every photo shoot and runway show (Wissinger, 2015) because they have had to take charge of their appearance by relying on their own resources. Many Black models report that professional makeup artists do not have the tools or skills to make up Black skin, which is one of the actual reasons the industry avoids Black models (Wissinger, 2015).

While limited numbers of Black models have been on the runway since the 1960s, women of color remain unacknowledged by the beauty industry even though they spend more time, energy and resources on managing their appearances (Reed & Medvedev, 2018). In this context, it is understandable that Rihanna's active participation in trying to find solutions suggests to her fans that she is committed to providing a platform for women of color that goes beyond the 'model types.'

While Black women have been ready to put in the labor needed for a 'perfect face,' the market, driven by White exclusionary beauty norms, has not met their needs. Rihanna's physical and emotional involvement in the beauty industry goes beyond commercial goals; she wants to be perceived as part of her community. Rihanna emphasizes that she has been brought up by Black women and therefore has their best interests at heart. Her line represents a social agenda: it seeks to make the realm of beauty more inclusive and attainable to women of color at all class levels. Despite being a true capitalist businesswoman, she instinctively represents an essentially Black feminist standpoint which prioritizes Black women's collective wellbeing and seeks concrete solutions to benefit the community.

Conclusion

Historically, societies have used beauty to draw boundaries around self-worth. Meeting White beauty standards can make or break opportunities for women of color. Glamour and managing one's appearance with cosmetics constitute a significant part of Rihanna's identity. When Rihanna conceptualized her beauty brand, she envisioned a product reminiscent of the makeup she loves and wants to wear. Though Fenty Beauty is not the first beauty brand to offer multiple shades of foundation, it is one of the first brands created by a Black woman for both "the pale girls and the dark-skinned girls" (Fenty Beauty by Rihanna, 2017).

Black celebrities such as Beyoncé, Queen Latifah, and Janelle Monae have also collaborated with major beauty brands like L'Oréal and Covergirl. But, unlike Fenty Beauty, their collaborations with the beauty industry come and go, based on perceptions of the strength of Black women's buying power by the industry. In contrast, Rihanna has remained committed to serving the interests of women of color.

Beauty can seem like a superficial issue to some, but in the historical context of the Black American experience, it is not. Black women have been repeatedly denied the ability to fashion their own appearance. Rihanna takes a political stance by acknowledging and boosting Black women's beauty. To offer cosmetics that are 'good enough' for Black women reinforces the notion that White women's beauty should remain the base measurement for the standard of beauty. By offering multiple products for diverse skin tones, Rihanna has started a beauty revolution with Fenty Beauty, leading to a confident and empowered female consumer of color.

References

Carroll, A. (2009). Brand communications in fashion categories using celebrity endorsement. *Journal of Brand Management, 17,* 146-158.

Collins, P. H. (2002). *Black feminist thought: Knowledge, consciousness, and the politics of empowerment.* New York: Routledge.

Conti, S. & Naughton, J. (2013. February 20). MAC joins forces with Rihanna. *Women's Wear Daily, 205*(36), 6.

Fenty Beauty. [@fentybeauty]. (2017, Oct 21). [Rihanna calls for a new generation of beauty]. https://www.instagram.com/p/BahkwaFl8Tw/?taken-by=fentybeauty

Fenty Beauty by Rihanna. (2017, September 8). Fenty face: The secret to Rihanna's killer radiance | Fenty Beauty [Video file]. Retrieved from https://www.youtube.com/watch?v=a-pryeiR6GA

Lowman, V. (2015, Jul 29). Everything you need to know about your skin's undertone. *Essence.* Retrieved from https://www.essence.com/beauty/makeup/everything-you-need-know-about-your-skins-undertone/

Marine, B. (2018, Jul 9). Kylie Jenner explained her decision to remove her lip fillers. *W Magazine.* Retrieved from https://www.wmagazine.com/story/kylie-jenner-old-lips

McCracken, G. (1989). Who is the celebrity endorser? Cultural foundations of the endorsement process. *Journal of Consumer Research*, 16, 310-321.

Morel, C. (2017, Sept 27). Rihanna quickly shuts down this makeup brand's shade against Fenty Beauty. *Bravo.* Retrieved from http://www.bravotv.com/blogs/rihanna-quickly-shuts-down-this-makeup-brands-shade-against-fenty-beauty

Newholm, T. & Hopkinson, G. C. (2009). I just tend to wear what I like: Contemporary consumption and the paradoxical construction of individuality. *Marketing Theory, 9*, 439-462.

Nye, J. (2004). *Soft power: The means to success in world politics*. New York: Public Affairs.

Reed, J., and Medvedev, K. (2018). The beauty divide: Black millennial women seek agency with Makeup Art Cosmetics. In A. Lynch & K. Medvedev (Eds.), *Fashion, agency and empowerment*. London: Bloomsbury. (pp. 11-27).

Schaefer, K. (2016, Oct 21). Kylie Jenner built a business empire out of lip kits and fan worship. *Vanity Fair.* Retrieved from https://www.vanityfair.com/style/2016/10/kylie-jenner-lip-kits-seed-beauty-colourpop

Thomas, S. (2014). Celebrity in the 'Twitterverse': History, authenticity, and the multiplicity of stardom. Situating the 'newness' of Twitter. *Celebrity Studies, 5*(3), 242-255.

Vogue. (2018a, May 3). Rihanna's epic 10-minute guide to going out makeup | Vogue | Beauty secrets [Video file]. Retrieved from https://www.youtube.com/watch?v=KONe4SNFA64&t=11s

Vogue. (2018b, June 27). Kylie Jenner's guide to lips, brows, confidence | Beauty secrets | Vogue [Video file]. Retrieved from https://www.youtube.com/watch?v=vCJ6U7mQmYw

Wissinger, E. A. (2015). *This year's model: Fashion, media, and the making of glamour.* New York: New York University Press.

Snooki Has #noshame: Representations and Redefinitions of Celebrity, Beauty, and Empowerment on Instagram

Victoria Kannen

Abstract. While some may see beauty practices as largely unchallenged in the last 30 to 50 years, social media has impacted the ways in which beauty imagery is discussed and circulated for wider audiences than we have known in the past. Currently, celebrity culture has begun to flaunt the ways in which bodies are modified – breast and butt implants, lip fillers, waist minimizers, and so on are now commonplace discussions on social media for some celebrities. In this chapter, I explore how a specific temporary practice of beautification – lip filling – relates to how social media can foster dialogues of shame and exoticization, while also positioning the body as a site for potential resistance to white-centric beauty ideals. Through discussion of shame and beautification, I address a celebrity – Nicole Polizzi, aka Snooki – and analyze imagery from her Instagram account to underscore the role of celebrity, social media, and the potential for reclamation of the self.

Keywords: Snooki, shame, Instagram, empowerment, beauty.

Introduction

In the age of the Kardashians, mainstream Western beauty practices have begun to shift. While feminist scholars, such as Susan Bordo, Jean Kilbourne, and Naomi Wolf have been critical of mainstream beauty practices for decades, social media and the #MeToo movement are impacting the ways in which beauty imagery is discussed and circulated for wider audiences than we have known in the past. As an example, for decades, women (and some men) have been surgically altering their bodies and the vast majority of these beauty modifications have been undertaken in secret (Northrop 2012). It has been a societal expectation to hide the fact that these procedures happen. We expect bodies to be able to espouse embodied *lies* in order to 'pass' as lucky and/or natural when they are deemed to conform to the ideals of beauty. However, the practices themselves have become commonplace, so much so that authors such as Bernadatte Wegenstein (2012) argue that our culture now uses a "cosmetic gaze," whereby our culture expects us to look at each other's bodies as neoliberal sites of improvement which are simply awaiting a procedural and surgical modification.

Currently, celebrity culture has begun to flaunt the ways in which bodies are modified – breast and butt implants, lip fillers, waist minimizers, and so on are now common-place discussions on social media for some celebrities. Celebrity culture directly influences the culture of social media in which many of us, and the vast majority of youth, participate. It is easy to break this down using Esther Dyson's notion of the "attention economy." For those active on social media, discourses of the feminine body on being thin, stylized, made up, and so on are pervasive and can be rewarded through *likes*, shares, and positive commentary as the attention of others is what drives this economy.

In this chapter, I explore how a specific temporary practice of beautification – lip filling – relates to how social media can foster dialogues of shame and exoticization, while also positioning the body – the celebrity body, in specific – as a site for potential resistance to white-centric beauty ideals. Following a brief review of the literature on shame and beautification, I discuss a celebrity – Nicole Polizzi – and analyze imagery published on her Instagram account, so as to underscore the role of celebrity, social media, and the potential for redefinition of the self.

Lip augmentation, which is more commonly known as lip filling, is a type of non-surgical cosmetic procedure that alters the appearance of lips by increasing their fullness through enlargement using some form of dermal fillers. This form of beautification practice has drastically increased in popularity due in large part to the platform of the Kardashian/Jenners and their participation in the practice (Sastre, 2014). Women disciplining their bodies using cosmetic procedures is certainly not a new practice, and the discourses of hard-work and exercise are all still in effect for women who want to meet the feminine ideal. However, the significance of celebrities explicitly acknowledging these practices of body work on social media deserves cultural consideration. Some celebrities not only admit/confess (as tabloid publications refer to it) but openly acknowledge surgically and procedurally altering their bodies. Do these presentations of self shift our understandings of beauty, identity, and self-worth? As noted in a *People* magazine article, Kylie Jenner's plastic surgeon Simon Ourian claims, "I had treated hundreds of celebrities before but very few of them were bold enough to share their [cosmetic surgery] secrets with such transparency. Her influence was much that what was once a taboo has now become a bragging right" (Kirkpatrick 2017, n.p.). We live in a culture where full celebrity confessions (mostly on social media) are seemingly required. Through social media, celebrities 1) demonstrate how they work hard – through exercise, eating well, drinking detox teas, taking supplements; 2) fill up – pop in for botox, lip filling, and be uncomfortable in waist trainers/corsets and, simultaneously, 3) sell products, ideals, and earn money from those confessions.

Shameful, Shameless

Angela McRobbie provides us with a useful concept – "the perfect." In her work, she explores the way that women govern and regulate themselves (drawing heavily on Michel Foucault's idea of governmentality and the body), in order to strive for the perfect in their lives. McRobbie states, "[b]y the perfect I mean a heightened form of self-regulation based on an aspiration to some idea of the 'good life'" (2015, p. 9). It is through self-monitoring, body work, and cosmetic surgery that women can attempt to thwart their own failure of achieving ultimate femininity and no longer feel shame for the bodies that they do not desire. These physically painful procedures can be used to give the sense of 'being in control' and therefore have the effect of (seemingly) putting a woman in charge of her body and her own empowerment (McRobbie 2015).

Oftentimes, our social media feeds contribute to the ways in which we can shame ourselves and others for the presentations of self that we see online. Shame has been well-developed as a mechanism of control for women in order to discipline their bodies so as to meet cultural ideals (Orenstein 2016). Shame is a "self-feeling that is felt by and on the body," as Sara Ahmed (2004, p. 103) notes. Jessica Ringrose and Laura Harvey (2015) argue that body shaming and 'slut shaming' has historically been an integral component to the construction of sexuality as it relates to feminized bodies. In their study of young women sexting, they conclude that "[i]t did not seem possible for girls to inhabit a public digital space in which they could actively request, take, send or post 'sexy photos' of their own bodies without risk of sexual shaming" (Ringrose and Harvey 2015, p. 207). The assumption is that women of all ages recognize that they are always already in a relationship with shaming – either it has or it will happen.

Social media shaming often emerges so as to hail and/or shame women for their embodied choices and presentations of self. As Ahmed notes, "the very physicality of shame – how it works on and through bodies – means that shame also involves the de-forming and re-forming of bodily and social spaces" (2004, p. 103). The virtual space that social media finds itself in is in no way disconnected from the materiality of our bodies. Our online identities are simply an extension of our physicality and this reality and connection must be constantly reflected upon. Further, theorists on shame and the body, such as Luna Dolezal (2015), argue that shame is painfully internalized while inherently a social emotion. The pervasive use of social media enables the language of shame within the 'attention economy' to then quietly creep into our social lives without necessarily being explicit. As Dolezal notes, body shame is "[o]ften an invisible and silent force, it is unacknowledged, but lurking" (2015, p. xvi).

Snooki and the Power of Celebrity

While Kim Kardashian West is perhaps the most recognizable and vocal celebrity regarding the presentation of self and the body on social media, I am more interested in a different American reality television and social media celebrity: Nicole Polizzi, also known as Snooki. I see Polizzi as less of a spectacle than Kardashian West in that she has less social and cultural recognition, but is still highly connected online in terms of followers and exposure on media platforms. Polizzi attempts to embody a more 'normal' and 'relatable' celebrity branding and, for this reason, I analyze a small, but emblematic sample of Polizzi's Instagram representations in terms of what they teach us about persona branding in this current cultural climate.

Polizzi rose to fame on the MTV reality show *The Jersey Shore* (and has also appeared on *Jersey Shore: Family Vacation*, 2018-present). The original show debuted in 2009 and, immediately, Polizzi was the standout. She was brash, outlandish, sexual, and was usually referred to as a 'sloppy mess' amongst many other gendered, sexualized, and classed vitriol (Horyn, 2010). As the show ended and she began a less popular spin-off, her image also began to change. She got married, had two children, and her celebrity presence now largely comes from appearing on Instagram, Snapchat, YouTube, and other internet broadcasts. The focus of her work is also on being a businesswoman - she has a clothing line, a crafting business, and a tanning collection, in addition to the various video episodes and guest-appearances that she shares across numerous platforms. Stephanie Patrick argues that the representations of 'Snooki' that proliferate characterize her as a post-feminist ambivalent character, who, among other characterizations, is "a woman who is always forced to choose between sex and proper womanhood" (2017, p. 185). Polizzi is caught within a representation that is so complex that in addition to the characterizations noted above, she is currently always already emphasizing her role as a mother and her transforming body. These are not in any way disconnected. Part of her current branding is that she is a fit mom; she has written books about this fitness and posts updates on her body work for her 12+ million followers on Instagram, as well as across her other social media platforms on a daily basis.

The function of Instagram is key here. It is a social photography application and, in its design, Instagram enables celebrities to personalize their experience of social interaction with fans and followers. Posting pictures "instantly", it encourages a seemingly more authentic interaction and conveyance of one's identity curation. In January 2016, Polizzi used the hashtag #noshame and posted a photo to Instagram (see Photo 1). Her caption states: "Making my lips look fabulous for 2016! Thanks @drkassir for always being awesome ♥

#mommytouchup #noshame". Here, Polizzi anticipates that her post will garner negative reaction and she preempts this by incorporating the inclusion of #noshame. What is the relationship between a lack of shame and celebrity admissions of modified beauty? When exploring the online social commentary on Polizzi's body and self-presentation, there are comments vacillating from deeming her as grotesque: "leave your face alone – you look inhuman" to desirous: "you inspire me to be the best version of myself." The comments position Polizzi's choice to modify her lips as grotesque, yet compelling, while also beautiful and empowering.

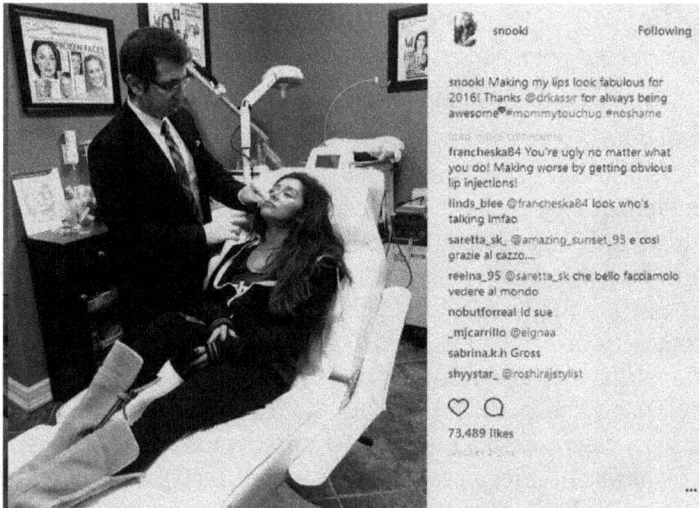

Photo 1. Credit: Instagram @snooki, January 4, 2016

Polizzi acknowledges that her celebrity presence is contradictory. Through her social media posts and videos, she often embraces the label of 'trash' that was profitable for her during her reign on reality television, while simultaneously and aggressively asserting her female power, branding power, and her pride in monogamy and motherhood. As many women, Polizzi's identity as spectacle fuelled fame. Initially, she was presented as having a body out of control, larger, yet petite, trashy, sexually available, and therefore comical and shameful. However, as seen in Photo 2, she now presents her body as powerful, strong, full, yet thin through her own control, and – perhaps most important to this discussion – as shame*less*.

It could be argued that Polizzi's presentation of self speaks directly to a post-feminist cultural moment where feminine empowerment is seen to be within the grasp of online fitness inspiration or "fitspo" imagery (Santarossa et al. 2016). The pushback against celebrity brandings such as Polizzi's from the

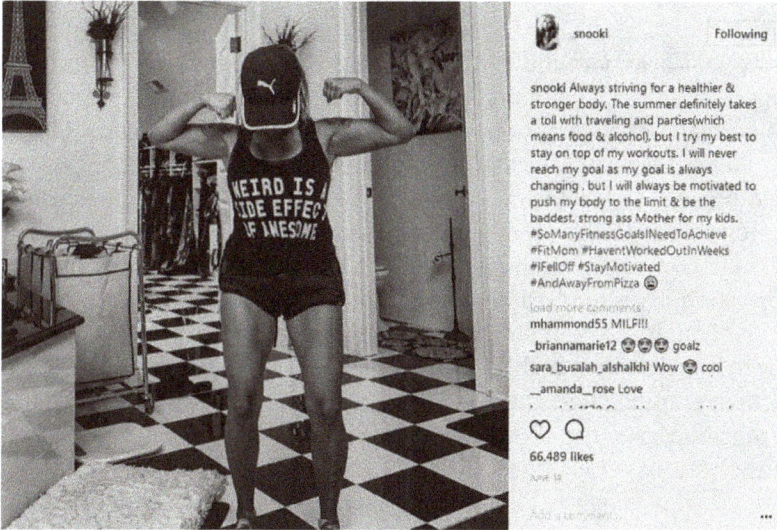

Photo 2. Credit: Instagram @snooki, June, 2017

feminist community speaks to the ways in which what is often viewed as 'superficial' celebrity culture and not worthy of scholarly consideration are also the spaces where cultural transmission of crucial ideas – such as #noshame – are currently taking place. Regardless of whether Polizzi would identify herself as a feminist, as a member of the "fitspo" community, or so on, I interpret the ways in which she characterizes herself as shame*less* as worthy of feminist attention.

Shame, as it relates to beauty, focuses not on the body work that has been undertaken as wrong or bad but rather on the self; as if the person is wrong or is now something bad because of the body work that they did OR because they do not shame others for that work. Shame is extremely debilitating because "it's the entire self that is painfully scrutinized and negatively evaluated" (Tangney 1996, p. 743). To announce oneself as shameless (as Polizzi does), speaks to an internal strength of character when one is seen to be participating in a practice that they could be and are shamed for, but has internal strength to refuse that shaming practice. Polizzi is both giving instruction to her followers – do not shame – while simultaneously announcing that there is no shame in what she is participating. Here, we see the complex relationship that we can have to empowerment: to be empowered can come from acknowledging that "the perfect" is not natural, but rather "the perfect" can come from a (potentially problematic) place of our choosing.

Privilege, Appropriation, and Commodification

The ideals of beauty in the West are intrinsically bound to the privileging of whiteness, thinness, symmetry, and youth. Cultural appropriation is a subject that is intimately tied to notions of lip filling and the embracing of 'Blackness' in this cultural moment. Richard A. Rogers argues, "[c]ultural appropriation, defined broadly as the use of a culture's symbols, artifacts, genres, rituals, or technologies by members of another culture, is inescapable when cultures come into contact, including virtual or representational contact. Cultural appropriation is also inescapably intertwined with cultural politics" (2006, p. 474). Although contemporary lip filling practices, predominantly seen practiced by celebrities such as Kylie Jenner, have become common-place, this aesthetic was often derided in the 1990s. The practice particularly led to racial discrimination against black women who bore larger lips naturally. Nevertheless, as Jess Lawrence states, "[t]he media will praise white celebrities who enhance their lips as 'trendsetters' and 'influencers' while emulating something for which black people have received hate and discrimination. For us, this aesthetic is not a trend but a representation of our race and culture" (2017, n.p.). While my analysis here is not of the merits of lip filling itself, but rather how social media practices enable various forms of empowerment through self-presentation, it is necessary to acknowledge how the practice itself could be undermining the very claims to empowerment that Polizzi's #noshame might be addressing. Empowerment – in this characterization – may come at the expense of racialized bodies and, therefore, does not speak to an intersectional feminist idea of empowerment.

A discussion of exoticization and cultural appropriation is important to this analysis as the ideals of beauty may be bound to notions of whiteness, thinness, and youth, but there have been dominant discourses as of late that express body types that diverge from this privileged ideal. While there are clear connections that can be made between the influence of celebrities such as Beyoncé, Jennifer Lopez, and Nicki Minaj, and the fetishization of the Other, it is important to also speak to the ways that body filling and the idealization of bodily curves can work as an active agent to push against and resist the status quo of thin, white-centric beauty that dominates high-fashion and mainstream popular culture. As Polizzi was adopted from Chile and raised in an Italian-American family, her non-white embodiment alongside her body work, adds commentary and social resistance to these white-centred ideals.

The flip side to this discussion of empowerment is the brand promotion that is embedded within this imagery. On social media, when a trusted celebrity endorses a product or a person, the level of interaction is markedly different than in a magazine ad, of course. Social media enables a one-to-one approach where advertising messages can be calibrated for the celebrity who is endorsing a product (Wood and Burkhalter, 2014). For example, Polizzi's discussion of her lip filling is simultaneously endorsing her plastic surgeon. Instagram enables these interactions to appear spontaneous, less commercial and perhaps more authentic or organic and thus more credible because she is no longer selling the 'trash' aesthetic. A sample of her Instagram stories from January 2019 shows her and her children in her mansion, promoting products from her fashion line, and selling VIP tickets to an event at her store The Snooki Shop, where she states, 'There will be champagne! Shopping! Yas queen!" (Instagram 2019). This level of intertwining consumerism and celebrity can have many neoliberal consequences: The brand familiarity of Polizzi may begin to exist alongside the brand familiarity of plastic surgery, detox teas she drinks, a purse she wants to sell in the store that she owns, and the body work that she is promoting. However, my analysis here has demonstrated that she is not only selling material goods as she is simultaneously exploring the ethics of shaming, shifting identities, and glamour.

Conclusion

Have these bodily presentations begun to allow for a wider variety of expressions of gendered beauty? Or, will the open dialogues surrounding bodily work further persuade women to feel compelled to participate? Elizabeth Wissinger (2015) argues that "glamour labor" – the work of self-styling, curating a 'look,' and building an image and identity – has become an integral part of our daily lives through the technology of social media. While she mostly focuses on the embodied work of fashion models, much can be said for the ways in which non-celebrities also attempt to achieve this unrealistic ideal. The ethics of beauty practices, social media, and the role of shame are pedagogically useful to consider as these practices of beautification exist along a continuum of hybrid identities and expressions of fluid gender. These ideas are fundamental to explore with a generation of predominantly young women and gender fluid youth who live alongside – and create their own identities – in response to this imagery.

Celebrity culture is commonly dismissed as meaningless or trivial. The narcissism that is expressed on social media might be characterized as a social ill, but these practices of self-presentation are not going anywhere. Millions upon millions of people emulate the social media behaviors of celebrities where they curate their own takes on gender, beauty, and body modification. The *likes* that we generate function as a social currency of acceptance, self-expression, and they advance understandings of ourselves to ourselves and to other people. If we consider each Instagram post as culturally pedagogical in its teachings about the shifting understandings of body work, then we can begin to recognize the possibilities of a shamelessness existence within this attention economy.

References

Ahmed, S. (2004). *The cultural politics of shame*. Edinburgh: Edinburgh University Press.

Dolezal, L. (2015). *The body and shame: Phenomenology, feminism, and the socially shaped body*. New York: Lexington.

Dyson, E. (2013). The rise of the attention economy. *The Independent*. https://www.independent.co.ug/rise-attention-economy/

Horyn, Cathy. (2010). Snooki's time. *The New York Times*. July 23, 2010. Retrieved from https://www.nytimes.com/2010/07/25/fashion/25Snooki.html

Kirkpatrick, E. (2017). Kylie Jenner's lips inspired copycat procedures. *People Magazine*. Retrieved from http://people.com/style/kylie-jenner-plastic-surgery-lips-trend/

Lawrence, J. (2017). The appropriation of fuller lips. Retrieved from http://www.gal-dem.com/appropriation-fuller-lips/

McRobbie, A. (2015). Note on the perfect: Competitive femininity in neoliberal times. *Australian Feminist Studies*, 30 (83), 3-20.

Northrop, J. (2012). *Reflecting on cosmetic surgery: Body image, shame and narcissism*. New York: Routledge.

Orenstein, P. (2016). *Girls & sex: Navigating the complicated new landscape*. New York: HarperCollins.

Patrick, S. (2017). "I want my Snooki": MTV's failed subjects and post-feminist ambivalence in and around the Jersey Shore. *Feminist Media Studies*, 17 (2), 181-197.

Polizzi, N. (2017). Instagram Account (@snooki). Photographs.

Ringrose, J., and Harvey, L. (2015). Boobs, back-off, six packs and bits: Mediated body parts, gendered reward, and sexual shame in teens' sexting image. *Continuum: Journal of Media & Cultural Studies*, 29 (2), 205-217.

Rogers, R. A. (2006). From cultural exchange to transculturation: A review and reconceptualization of cultural appropriation. *Communication Theory*, 16, 474-503.

Santarossa, S., Coyne, P., Lisinski, C., and Woodruff, S.J. (2016). #fitspo on Instagram: A mixed-methods approach using Netlytic and photo analysis, uncovering the online discussion and author/image characteristics. *Journal of Health Psychology*, https://doi.org/10.1177/1359105316676334

Sastre, A. (2014). Hottentot in the age of reality TV: Sexuality, race, and Kim Kardashian's visible body. *Celebrity Studies*, 5 (1-2), 123-137.

Tangney, J. P. (1996). Conceptual and methodological issues in the assessment of shame and guilt. *Behaviour Research & Therapy*, 34 (9), 741-754.

Wegenstein, B. (2012). *The cosmetic gaze: Body modification and the construction of beauty*. Cambridge: MIT Press.

Wissinger, E. (2015). *This year's model: Fashion, media, and the making of glamour*. New York: NYU Press.

Wood, N. T., and Burkhalter, J. N. (2014). "Tweet this, not that": A comparison between brand promotions in microblogging environments using celebrity and company-generated tweets. *Journal of Marketing Communications*, 20 (1-2), 129-146.

Part III:
Redefining Role Models in Celebrity Culture

Reframing Hollywood: Dissecting the Celebrity-led #timesup Initiative

Nikki Soo and Claudia Ferreira

Abstract. Widespread support from beyond the movie industry after Harvey Weinstein's allegations fuelled a new political movement that led to the exposure of previously unknown misogynistic behaviour by beloved entertainment personalities, and to a reframing of Hollywood's awards season. Unlike typical celebrity activism, this movement stands out with celebrities as the driving force behind this cause. We focus on the 2018 Golden Globes, an event notable for the coordinated rejection and fight against sexual misconduct, in Hollywood and beyond. Unlike previous years where glamour took centre stage, this ceremony was marked by celebrity activism, subsequently impacting Twitter, where the hashtags #metoo, #timesup, and #whyiwearblack were trending on 7th January 2018. This paper presents an analysis of celebrity tweets with the hashtag #timesup during the Golden Globes red carpet, arguing that, in times of political disengagement, celebrities' re-branding as forces for social change can result in widespread connective and collective action.

Keywords: activism, celebrities, sexual harassment, social movement, Twitter.

Introduction

In the aftermath of the #metoo movement[1], Hollywood stars continued their coordinated effort to counter systemic female sexual abuse and harassment in the workplace. The "Time's Up" initiative was announced in the New York Times on 1st January 2018 through an open letter signed by hundreds of women in the movie industry. This initiative includes a legal fund to help victims of sexual harassment, making the Hollywood-led movement against sexual harassment more inclusive and open to the general public. This chapter's analysis focuses on the first #timesup-related event – the 2018 Golden Globes ceremony, in particular, the red carpet component of the evening. We demonstrate how celebrities used this opportunity to *re*frame their personal branding as they were viewed at a typically glamorous event that often focused on what they wore. While award ceremonies are often fraught with scandal (English, 2005), these actresses drew attention to their protest against the unspoken systemic sexual harassment experienced by women, including

---

[1] In October 2017, media mogul Harvey Weinstein's revelations resulted in a viral hashtag #metoo used by victims of sexual harassment to share their experiences.

themselves, not only because they chose to wear only black to the red carpet, but also because they brought activists as their dates for the night. As a result, actions and tweets with the hashtag #timesup, along with #whywewearblack and #metoo updated over the course of the red carpet, paved the way for celebrities to be viewed as activists driving real change.

This chapter will first consider literature on celebrity activism and the role of Twitter in connective and collective action. It will then discuss the theory and method, before investigating findings from the tweets collected. Finally, we will discuss how reframing of celebrities' personal branding towards one of an activist who enhances democratic behavior.

Literature Review

Recent research suggests traditional forms of political participation are in decline, and concerned citizens are finding new and innovative ways of engaging in politics. Bauman (2000), Bang (2003), and Keane (2009) argue that contemporary political participation is less associated with socio-demographic factors, and that information technologies play an increasingly important role in the process of collective action. Social media brings citizens with similar concerns together and enables activists to communicate with a worldwide audience by lowering barriers or dependence from traditional media platforms (Chadwick, 2013). In this context, celebrity activism is now associated with the creation of new pathways to attention for dissents (Tufekci, 2013), and enhancement of democratic behavior. This contradicts previous notions that celebrity activism is self-interested (Boorstin, 1971; Alberoni, 1972; Mills, 1956; Meyer, 1995). The trajectory of the #metoo and #timesup initiatives implies that, when shared grievances exist, the general public supports the involvement of celebrities in the political sphere.

#TimesUp stands out as celebrities are not your run-of-the-mill celebvocates (Tsaliki, 2015). Based on the literature, we argue they are the driving force behind the movement as victims by using the Golden Globes, an event associated with fashion and glamour as a platform, rather than individuals supporting a good cause. This represents a re-branding of Hollywood stars as forces for social change, and the level of online engagement with the #timesup movement found in our research supports the notion that celebrities' political activism can have a positive effect in the age of political disenfranchisement. As Kaikati and Kaikati explain, "robust brands have always had to evolve to remain desirable" and celebrities are no different (2003:17). Considering the important role that brands play in our society as media of exchange (Giddens, 1991), celebrity brands are the "mediatized embodiment of market logics that reach into cultural fields and shared experience spinning them as everyday capacities to produce a common, branded, social world of being" (Brownlie et al., 2015). Drawing on the existing literature, our research asks, how did celebrities perceive and champion Time's Up in the context of the Golden Globes 2018?

Theory and Method

We drew on Entman's framing theory to demonstrate how celebrities sought to reframe how the Golden Globes award ceremony was perceived, along with their presence at the red carpet. Frames refer to the selection and emphasis of specific pieces of information to "promote a particular problem definition, casual interpretation, moral evaluation and/or treatment recommendation" (Entman, 1993: 52). These frames guide audiences' thinking by making some aspects of reality more memorable or meaningful. By offering an alternative meaning to the Golden Globes red carpet, celebrities challenged audience's dominant reading of the event.

Tweets from the evening of 7th January 2018 with the hashtags #timesup and #whywewearblack were scraped using Python. The total number of tweets collected was 16 643, and were organized according to their popularity (the number of favorites used as an indicator) and time posted. Next, we drew on two-stage sentiment analysis proposed by Hopkins and King (2010). The raw data was cleaned before it was coded by hand. Due to the large data sample, purposeful sampling was applied. Case selection is based on participant characteristics in data collection and the study's objectives (Patton 2002). This method was selected as most appropriate as it allows subtle nuances of tweets to emerge, despite the volume of data. As we are concerned with the role of celebrities, we considered tweets by celebrities in the top 1000 most popular tweets in our data, from 186 celebrity accounts. This was done with the use of a codebook with 11 questions that examined sentiment, positive prognosis, and blame attribution.

Lastly, researchers who draw on tweets are faced with complex ethical considerations regarding the private and public nature of the information presented. However, all tweets collected and examined in this paper were publicly available at the time of research, requiring no permission from Twitter account holders for analysis and publication.

Findings

During the red carpet of the 2018 Golden Globes, 28.85% of the 1000 most popular tweets were by celebrities, most with followings ranging from 500,000 to millions. Applying Entman's four framing functions to tweets by celebrities in attendance, we observed that Time's Up organizer's tweets fall into at least one of the categories described in Table 1.

Table1. Time's Up Initiative According to Entman

Entman's Framing Functions	Time's Up Tweets
Define a specific problem	Unspoken systemic sexual harassment, especially women
Diagnose a cause for the problem	Lack of support for victims to take their harassers into account, and fear of jeopardizing their career
Make a moral judgment on problem	This cannot continue and needs to be changed
Propose a solution	Emotional, financial, and professional support and encourage victims to come forward

Image 1 shows an example of a tweet by Brie Larson, a celebrity involved in bringing attention to the Time's Up initiative, that includes the four categories highlighted above:

Our sentiment analysis showed that 49.1% of tweets were neutral. Tweets coded as neutral predominantly stated facts, as demonstrated by this tweet from actress Emma Watson (Image 2). They do not reflect ambivalence, but instead, provide support for tweets with positive sentiments. 47.76% of celebrity tweets portrayed a positive sentiment towards the movement. Furthermore, 2.46% of positive tweets expressed urgency, emphasizing the importance of the movement and the change it stands for. While seemingly low, this indicates an understanding within the movement of the ambitious nature of their goal of toppling gender imbalance. However, we argue the large number of positive tweets indicate that these goals are not unattainable.

Image 1. Tweet from actress Brie Larson, posted 7th Jan 2018.

Image 2. Tweet from actress Emma Watson, posted 7 Jan 2018.

Finally, 3.16% conveyed negativity. These tweets were not negative towards the movement but expressed negativity towards the industry and how women were treated. Five actresses also blamed Hollywood's culture for the fact that so many women in the movie industry have had experiences of gender discrimination or sexual misconduct. While tweets from the general public placed blame mostly on public figures who also committed sexual misconduct, such as Woody Allen and his associates (Justin Timberlake and Blake Lively most commonly cited), Hollywood's elites seem to view their industry's permissive culture as the main cause for this widespread issue.

On the same night, celebrities also contributed to the virality of the #metoo movement by using it in the context of the protest to share their experiences of sexual assault. 13 tweets by celebrities sharing experiences of sexual misconduct outside and inside Hollywood gathered the attention of the main public who showed their solidarity by retweeting and favoriting these stories.

Actress Bella Thorne went viral after sharing a childhood experience of sexual assault, with her story retweeted a total of 4171 times and favorited by 24896 twitter users.

Furthermore, 27 celebrities communicated positive prognostics, sharing tweets expressing how hopeful they feel for the future of the movement and its ability to change our culture, and ultimately helping women to feel as safe as their male counterparts. One important example was a tweet by Kerry Washington championing the movement by explaining its potential to correct the imbalance of power in the workplace that still affects most women. This was retweeted 1968 times and favorited 7541 times, indicating the solidarity and support that this cause found on social media.

Analysis and Conclusion

With the use of Entman's framing theory, it can be observed that celebrities involved in the Time's Up initiative have sought to reframe not only their position as celebrities, but as activists seeking to establish solidarity and, subsequently, cause institutional change and enhance democratic behavior (Street, 2004). This constituted the highest peak of the first wave of contention for Time's Up, marked by a strong expansion of contention across social groups and sectors, transcending national borders and media platforms (Koopmans, 2004).

This reframing resulted in the potential to continuously impact public perception through ripples. The Time's Up initiative inspired well-attended marches and rallies on the 22th Jan 2018 in 36 cities, drawing tens of thousands of women in places such as London, New York, and Los Angeles. A further implication of this has meant the success of the celebrities' reframing could potentially change how the media industry in Hollywood operates, and empowering victims of sexual harassment in any other industries to hold their harassers accountable.

The re-branding of celebrities and Hollywood events as forces for social change can contribute to countering contemporary political apathy and disenfranchisement. As the night of the Golden Globes 2018 demonstrates, when celebrities share a common grievance with their audience, they can gather the support of the online community. This was done by establishing solidarity with calls to end systemic sexual assault and harassment in the workplace, observed in their viral tweets. This wave of solidarity then continued throughout the year and resulted in collective action, as the previously mentioned street protests demonstrate.

References

Alberoni, F. (1972). The Powerless 'Elite': Theory and Sociological Research on the Phenomenon of the Stars." pp. 75–98 in *Sociology of Mass Communications: Selected Readings*, edited by D. McQuail. Middlesex, UK: Penguin Books.

Bauman, Z. (2013). *Liquid modernity*. Cambridge, UK: Polity Press

Boorstin, D. (1971). *The Image: A Guide to Pseudo-events in America*. New York: Atheneum.

Brownlie, D., Hewer, P., & Kerrigan, F. (2015). Celebrity, Convergence and Transformation. *Journal of Marketing Management*, 31(5), 453-460.

Chadwick, A. (2017). *The hybrid media system: Politics and power*. Oxford University Press.

Dekker, P., & Uslaner, E. M. (2003). *Social capital and participation in everyday life*. Routledge.

English, J. F. (2005). *The Economy of Prestige: Prizes, Awards, and the Circulation of Cultural Value*, Harvard University Press.

Entman, R. (1993). Framing: Toward Clarification of a Fractured Paradigm, *Journal of Communication*, 43(3): 51-58.

Giddens, A. (1991). *Modernity and self-identity: Self and society in the late modern age*. Cambridge: Polity Press.

Hopkins, D. J., & King, G. (2010). A method of automated nonparametric content analysis for social science. *American Journal of Political Science*, 54(1), 229-247.

Kaikati, J. G., & Kaikati, A. M. (2003). A rose by any other name: rebranding campaigns that work. *Journal of Business Strategy*, 24(6), 17-23.

Keane, J. (2009). Monitory Democracy and media-saturated societies, *Griffith Review*, Edition 24: Participation Society. Available online at: http://www.griffithreview.com/edition-24-participation-society/222-essay/657.html.

Koopman, (2004). Protest in Time and Space: The Evolution of Waves of Contention in David Snow (2004) ed. *The Blackwell Companion to Social Movements*, Blackwell.

Meyer, D. S. (1995). The challenge of cultural elites: Celebrities and social movements. *Sociological Inquiry*, 65(2), 181-206.

Mills, C. W. (1956). *The power elite*. Oxford University Press.

Patton, M. Q. (2002). Two decades of developments in qualitative inquiry: A personal, experiential perspective. *Qualitative social work* 1(3), 261-283.

Tsaliki, L. (2015). "Tweeting the Good Causes": Social Networking and Celebrity Activism. A companion to celebrity, 235-257.

Tufekci, Z. (2013). "Not this one" social movements, the attention economy, and microcelebrity networked activism. *American Behavioral Scientist* 57(7), 848-870.

Emma Watson's 'The Press Tour': Fashion Activism as Personal Brand

Maureen Lehto Brewster

Abstract. Actress and activist Emma Watson pledged to wear only "green" – sustainably produced – clothing for her press appearances as of 2015. This chapter analyzes "The Press Tour," an Instagram account that she started in 2017 to document her sustainable style. Discursive analysis of her social media accounts, as well as an examination of her broader star image, suggests Watson is branding herself as a model of ethical glamour in the sustainable fashion community. This chapter examines "The Press Tour," and Watson's personal branding as ethical fashionista, as part of a connective action network (Bennett and Segerberg 2012), to unpack Watson's influence in the fashion industry.

Keywords: social media, branding, star image, sustainable fashion, connective action.

Introduction

As it has evolved into a major marketing hub, Instagram's fashion-oriented accounts are most often centered upon the promotion of advertising over activism, consumption over contemplation – an aesthetic economy built on an ever-expanding network of celebrity and self-constructed micro-celebrity figures known as "influencers." While many of these microcelebrity figures leverage their fame and following for what might be called "conventional" fashion – companies, designs, and practices that are not sustainable, ethical, or environmentally friendly – there is a growing community of influencers promoting these ideals on the photo-sharing social media application. A notable example is "The Press Tour" (TPT), founded in 2017 by actress and activist Emma Watson.[1] The account was originally created to document the outfits from Watson's press tour for the 2017 film *Beauty and the Beast*, though it continues to display and describe the clothing she has worn to public appearances after that tour – all of which are styled using sustainable, ethical, and/or eco-friendly fashion and beauty brands that have been verified by third-party firms.

This chapter uses The Press Tour as a lens to explore Watson's personal branding as a fashion activist, and to contextualize her social media practices

---

[1] See: https://www.instagram.com/the_press_tour

within both activist and influencer discourse on Instagram. Through an ethnographic study of two related and yet somewhat oppositional communities – "traditional" fashion influencers and sustainable fashion influencers – I will aim to unpack the visual and textual rhetoric of fashion activism on Instagram, and how the ethics of sustainable fashion are negotiated within this highly commodified, consumption-driven space. The chapter will evaluate Watson's social media practices on TPT and her related accounts alongside her offline star image, to better understand how they coalesce. Using Bennett and Segerberg's (2012) logic of connective action, it will ultimately question whether these branding strategies make her into an effective model of ethical glamour.

The Press Tour

Instagram's focus on relentless novelty and aspirational glamour makes it a murky territory for fashion activism, but there is a growing community of influencers and enthusiasts who have used the platform to promote sustainable and ethical fashion. Among the over 2M sustainable fashion accounts on Instagram, Emma Watson's The Press Tour is by far the best publicized, due to Watson's celebrity status as a star in two hugely successful franchises: WB's *Harry Potter* and Disney's *Beauty and the Beast*. Watson has three accounts attributed to her: her personal account (@emmawatson); Our Shared Shelf (@oursharedshelf), the official account for the feminist book club she founded in 2016; and The Press Tour, dedicated to sustainable, ethical fashion and beauty. TPT has 34 posts, making it the least active of Watson's accounts, but it has over 493k followers. Most of the images are red carpet photos and street style photos, the poses and framing of which mimic the "dynamic, candid" quality of street style photography as described by Luvaas (2016, 64-65). Apart from her penchant for rooftop pictures, most of these posts are nearly identical to many of the over 67 million tagged as "fashionblogger" on Instagram: with her hip often cocked, clad in designer clothing in perfectly lit, lush settings, and her gaze fixed beyond the camera, Watson epitomizes the visual discourse of fashion photography on Instagram.

The most-liked post, with over 492k views, is a short video from February 21, 2017, showing a series of photos documenting Watson's trip from Paris to London for her *Beauty and the Beast* (2017) press tour. The cover photo shows Watson at the top of an escalator, clutching a sleek black suitcase in one hand and a bouquet of red roses in the other. The origins of her all-black ensemble are detailed in the 332-word caption, naming not only the brand names, but also the materials and production process of everything from her jewelry to her boots. (Notably missing from this laundry list – to the frustration of a few commenters – is the leather Givenchy Horizon small bag seen in several photos, perhaps because it is not created with the same ethics as the other pieces.[2]) The caption begins with a light, conversational greeting – "Merci beaucoup Paris for the wonderful start to the @beautyandthebeast tour!" – and a reference to the film. Two emojis (a French flag and a rose, very Belle) serve as a divider between this more traditional, Instagram-friendly caption and the decidedly pedagogical description of her clothing that follows. For example: when describing her bodysuit, Watson not only mentions that the brand – Woron – is "slow fashion," but also explains that it is made from "Lenzing Modal® fabric, a fibre made from beech wood sourced from sustainable forestry plantations in Europe" (The Press Tour, 2017). Her socks are made from certified organic bamboo in a zero-waste factory; her jacket is vegan leather Stella McCartney; even her eyebrow gel is certified cruelty-free.[3] TPT's divided caption format – part bubbly, influencer-style greeting and part sustainable fashion class – continues throughout the account.

These decidedly educational captions are a departure from the typical tone and goal of fashion influencer discourse on Instagram. Traditional fashion posts are often composed to promote the style of the influencer and the clothing they wear; this is accomplished through appropriating the visual language of street style and celebrity, as Luvaas (2016) and Chafkin (2016) describe: some poses appropriate a "straight up" style, remediating images of models in editorial fashion photography, while more candid "paparazzi-style" images connote the fame and glamour of an Insta-famous lifestyle. Watson's posts on TPT tend toward the latter. Her posts also utilize what Abidin (2015) notes are "advertorial" style captions: "a pastiche of 'advertisement' and 'editorial'" that are "highly personalized, opinion-laden promotions of products/services."

Images on the account are tagged so that followers can access brand information and shop their looks. Additional hashtags on posts help connect the account to the larger sustainable fashion community; one example is

---

[2] The House of Givenchy designed Watson's red carpet gown for the New York City premiere of *Beauty and the Beast* in collaboration with Livia Firth's consultancy firm Eco-Age; in an interview with *Teen Vogue* about the gown, a source at Givenchy revealed that the house also created a faux leather version of the Horizon bag especially for her, "to complement her sustainable wardrobe." It is unclear if the bag in this series of photos is this version or the original, leather version. See: Faith Cummings, "Emma Watson's *Beauty and the Beast* Red Carpet Designers Talk Sustainability in Fashion," *Teen Vogue*, 2017, https://www.teenvogue.com/gallery/emma-watson-beauty-and-the-beast-eco-friendly-givenchy-elie-saab-emilia-wickstead.

[3] Consultancy firm Eco-Age verifies the background information about her clothing's production, while Content Beauty verifies her beauty products. See: https://www.instagram.com/the_press_tour.

"#30wears," which is used by users on Instagram to denote garments that have been worn multiple times. The tag seems to promote a more lasting relationship with clothing, as opposed to continually purchasing and wearing new pieces as many influencers and #ootd posts do. Watson uses the tag several times on TPT, often for pieces by designers that might not be explicitly eco-conscious, such as a pair of Oscar de la Renta trousers and Burberry silk pumps that she wears in a March 2017 post. This hashtag not only connects Watson's posts to the larger community of sustainable fashion advocates, but also demonstrates to followers how one can follow principles of said community without renovating their entire wardrobe. This is crucial because it models sustainable and ethical behavior that is not based on consumption, a rarity for Instagram.

The tag "#30wears" thus creates what Bennett and Segerberg (2012) call a "connective action network," a form of digital activism whereby "political content [is shared] in the form of easily personalized ideas" (p. 744). Another example is the tag "#whomademyclothes," which is organized by Fashion Revolution to highlight the plight of garment workers. Such tags are part call to action, part meme, and part collective organization, allowing participants from within and outside of the community to participate easily. While these tags may have originated with a specific organization, or find amplification from influencers like Watson, they take on a life of their own as "personal action frames" that are "inclusive," "easily personalized," and can be easily shared via communication technologies (ibid.). Following Bennett and Segerberg's logic of connective action, the hashtag "#30wears" is effective because it is "self-motivated (though not necessarily self-centered) sharing of already internalized or personalized ideas, plans, images, and resources with networks of others" (p. 753). The tag allows users to participate in a shared community action and promote their values in an easy and effective way.

Watson uses this and related tags to promote ethical principles and signify her participation in the connective action network of sustainable fashion on her account; however, her concurrent use of influencer imagery and rhetoric somewhat sanitizes those issues. Her "distracting performance of identity" (Tolentino, 2016) glosses over the structural inequalities and failures of the fashion system, and presents consumption as the primary solution – as if "*seeing* and purchasing" sustainable fashion is the same as changing those issues (Banet-Weiser, 2018, 4, original emphasis). The account thus urges followers to engage in "consumer citizenship" (Pham, 2011), framing their purchasing power as a political act of self-expression, freedom, and personal choice (Banet-Weiser, 2012; Duffy and Hund, 2015; Gill, 2007; McRobbie, 2004). In short, TPT's content often promotes glamour at the expense of more challenging ethical conversations.

The account therefore highlights one of the pitfalls of connective action: that the highly personalized and self-validating nature of these networks may not be "stable [or] capable of various kinds of targeted action" (Bennett and Segerberg, 2012, 752-754). Those same features, however, make it incredibly effective at promoting Watson as an activist. In the next section, I will discuss how TPT relies on Watson's star image (Dyer, 1998), and the parasocial relationships (Turner, 2001) between Watson and her fans, to fuel its connective action network and further spread Watson's ideals.

Ethical Glamour as Celebrity Brand

As Dyer (1998) describes, a celebrity's star image is constructed of a celebrity's various media texts to convey their identity and personality to consumers; Watson's star image is almost hyper-focused on fashion, feminism, and education, making her a particularly influential and trusted figure in the sustainable fashion community. She was appointed UN Goodwill Ambassador in 2014, and has spearheaded the UN Women's "HeForShe" campaign for gender equality in numerous events as well as on her own social media platforms. She is a graduate of Brown University with a degree in English literature; one of her Instagram accounts, @oursharedshelf, is a feminist book club. Watson is known as a "book fairy," and often leaves copies of the club's selections hidden around the world (Rahim, 2017). She has also been a vocal supporter of the "Time's Up" movement, not only via her social media presence but also by her fashion choices during the 2018 red carpet circuit (which were documented, naturally, on TPT). Her modeling work for high fashion brands such as Burberry and Chanel, as well as design collaborations with ethical fashion label People Tree, speak to her established expertise in the fashion industry. Meanwhile, her two best-known film roles are seen as intellectual, feminist icons in popular culture: Hermione Granger in *Harry Potter,* and Belle in *Beauty and the Beast*. These threads all come together to establish Watson's star image as feisty heroine, social activist, fashion model, and intellectual.

When viewed in light of these layered identities, TPT feels like a genuine effort to educate Watson's followers about more eco-conscious production and consumption of fashion. The account's use of visual and textual "influencer" strategies – Watson's editorial-style poses, brand tags and links, and advertorial captions – makes sustainable and ethical fashion visually appealing to consumers. However, the account is also a tool to promote Emma Watson, the celebrity. Sharing behind the scenes information about her outfits and press activities helps facilitate the "perceived interconnectedness" or one-sided, "parasocial connections" between Watson and her followers (Turner, 2001;

Abidin, 2015). Because social media appears to be a direct and authentic line of communication to the celebrity, it creates an illusion of intimacy that can be used to create and commodify parasocial relationships (Marwick & boyd, 2011; Meyers, 2009). By drawing upon that intimacy and authenticity, Watson is able to use TPT to reinforce her star image and brand herself as a model for ethical glamour. The network of connective action thus becomes a network for the proliferation of Watson's personal brand, enabling her image as fashion activist to solidify further within and beyond her social media network.

Conclusion

By appropriating the visual language of fashion influence, and using the text and content of posts as a personal action frame, accounts like TPT serve as much-needed models of sustainable, ethical fashion behavior, though it is difficult to say whether these oppositional discourses can gain traction among consumers (or indeed whether they are truly ethical, particularly when monetized). However, recent research indicates that "exposure to social media content about sustainable apparel is a direct and indirect predictor of intentions to buy sustainable apparel," though authors de Lenne and Vandenbosch also lament that "young consumers are rarely exposed to such media" (2017, 495).[4] It will also be crucial to offer representations of sustainable fashion both online and on the rack that are more accessible to consumers who are not thin, white, able-bodied and wealthy.

In the short term, TPT is clearly a platform for Emma Watson's personal branding as an activist. The account serves as a linchpin of her intersecting media texts, and therefore as a key site for the formation of her star image – where her identities as actress, activist, and fashion influencer coalesce. The formatting of her posts borrows from established activist and influencer strategies, enabling her to participate in a connective action network mobilized around her celebrity. The account's "behind the scenes" look into the red carpet also creates an "illusion of intimacy" for fans (Marwick & boyd, 2011), which strengthens both her parasocial connections with followers and her overall personal branding as an ethical fashion activist.

---

[4] This may be changing: celebrities such as Rosario Dawson and Rooney Mara are each co-founders of ethical fashion brands, while Jessica Alba's Honest Company offers "clean" beauty, baby, and personal care products. See: Kristen Tauer and Leigh Nordstrom, "Celebrities and Models Supporting Sustainability," *WWD*, December 20, 2018, https://wwd.com/eye/people/celebrities-models-actors-sustainability-environmental-activism-1202938605/ (accessed January 15, 2019).

What makes Emma Watson's brand so strong is its repetition across multiple, interconnected social media accounts, as well as in her media appearances and professional activities. Her consistent online support of ethical fashion, combined with her offline work in acting and activism, do not just make her an intriguing case study – they position her as a powerful voice for the sustainable fashion community.

References

Abidin, C. (2015). Communicative Intimacies: Influencers and Perceived Interconnectedness. *ADA: A Journal of Gender, New Media, and Technology,* No. 8. Retrieved from doi:10.7264/N3MW2FFG.

Banet-Weiser, S. (2012). *Authentic™: The politics of ambivalence in a brand culture.* New York, NY: NYU Press.

—— (2018). *Empowered: Popular Feminism and Popular Misogyny.* Durham, N.C.: Duke University Press.

Bennett, W. L. & Segerberg, A. (2012). The Logic of Connective Action. *Information, Communication & Society*, 15 (5), 739-768.

Chafkin, M. (2016). Confessions of an Instagram Influencer. Bloomberg Businessweek. Retrieved from https://www.bloomberg.com/news/features/2016-11-30/confessions-of-an-instagram-influencer

Cummings, F. (2017). Emma Watson's *Beauty and the Beast* Red Carpet Designers Talk Sustainability in Fashion. *Teen Vogue,* April 22. Retrieved from https://www.teenvogue.com/gallery/emma-watson-beauty-and-the-beast-eco-friendly-givenchy-elie-saab-emilia-wickstead.

de Lenne, O. & Vandenbosch, L. (2017). Media and sustainable apparel buying intention. *Journal of Fashion Marketing and Management: An International Journal,* 21 (4), 483-498.

Duffy, B. E. and Hund, E. (2015). "Having it All" on Social Media: Entrepeneurial Femininity and Self-Branding Among Fashion Bloggers. *Social Media & Society,* 1 (2): 1-11.

Dyer, R. (1998). *Stars,* 2nd ed. London: BFI.

Gill, R. (2007). Postfeminist media culture: Elements of a sensibility. *European Journal of Cultural Studies,* 10, 147–166.

Luvaas, B. (2016). *Street Style: An Ethnography of Fashion Photography*. London and New York: Bloomsbury.

Marwick, A. & boyd, d. (2011). To See and Be Seen: Celebrity Practice on Twitter. *Convergence: The International Journal of Research into New Media Technologies,* 17 (2), 139-158.

McRobbie, A. (2004). Post-feminism and popular culture. *Feminist Media Studies* 4 (3), 255–264.

Meyers, E. (2009). "Can You Handle My Truth?": Authenticity and the Celebrity Star Image. *The Journal of Popular Culture,* 42 (5).

Pham, M. (2011). The Right to Fashion in the Age of Terrorism. *Signs,* 36 (2), 385-410.

Rahim, L. (2017). Emma Watson's army of 'book fairies' are leaving novels in public spaces all over the world. *The Telegraph,* March 8. Retrieved from https://www.telegraph.co.uk/women/life/international-womens-day-2017-emma-watsons-army-book-fairies/.

Tauer, K. and Nordstrom, L. (2018). Celebrities and Models Supporting Sustainability. *WWD,* December 20. Retrieved from https://wwd.com/eye/people/celebrities-models-actors-sustainability-environmental-activism-1202938605/.

Tolentino, J. (2016). How "Empowerment" Became Something for Women to Buy. *The New York Times Magazine,* April 12. Retrieved from https://www.nytimes.com/2016/04/17/magazine/how-empowerment-became-something-for-women-to-buy.html.

Turner, G. (2001). *Understanding Celebrity.* London: SAGE.

How Can a Supermodel Influence Social, Environmental, and Animal Causes through Social Media? A Case Study with the Brazilian Supermodel Gisele Bündchen

Douglas Silva and Renata Prado

Abstract. This paper aims to investigate how celebrities use social media for activism. We conducted a case study in order to analyze Brazilian supermodel Gisele Bündchen, the world's highest paid model from 2002 to 2016. We gathered all her Facebook data from her first post in March 2011 until February 2018 and classified every Facebook post from January 1, 2017 to January 1, 2018 in order to analyze how she uses social media and the engagement of Gisele Bündchen's followers with her social/environmental/animal causes posts compared to her non-social/environmental/animal posts. We concluded that Gisele Bündchen's followers are not primarily interested in her activism posts, therefore, by engaging in activism through social media, she endorses activist causes and reaches millions of followers who were not primarily interested in this kind of information, making a great impact on activism.

Keywords: activism, social media, Facebook, supermodel, Gisele Bündchen.

Introduction

In the 1990s Giselle Bündchen was nothing more than a happy, healthy, tall, skinny, volleyball-loving, animal-adoring teenager living in the south of Brazil, in a small village of 10,000 people (Rolling Stone, 2000). The woman called by Rolling Stone (2000) "the most beautiful girl in the world" and by Vanity Fair (2013) "the fashion reigning supermodel," had never seen a fashion magazine until she was 13. She only started her modeling career due to a free 25-hour bus trip from her small town to São Paulo in 1995, attracted by a chance to visit a big city for the first time. She was eating her first meal at a McDonald's when a modeling agent saw her. In the first months, people didn't think she was pretty enough, but in 1997 she was selected for two runway shows in London (including Alexander McQueen's), Dolce & Gabbana and Versace catwalks (in Milan), and French Vogue put her on the cover and one magazine after another did the same. Then she did advertising campaigns for Dior, Balenciaga, Givenchy, and Ralph Lauren. At that time, she was wealthy enough to turn down work. Then she signed a five-year contract with Victoria's Secret (Vanity Fair, 2013). Today she is a top contemporary celebrity. Her successful supermodel career, her millionaire contracts, and her popularity on social media confirms her fame (Fortune, 2018). In 2007 she was considered the 16th richest woman in the entertainment industry (Forbes, 2018). She was the highest paid model from 2002 to 2016 (Forbes Brasil, 2018) and has been on more than 500 magazine covers during her career (Voguepedia, 2018). She was also recognized for her social and environmental work, earning the Global Citizen Award in 2011 (United Nations Environment Programme, 2018), International Green Awards also in 2011 (International Green Awards, 2018), and the Green Carpet Fashion Award in 2017 (Eco-Age, 2018).

This study aims to identify how someone like Gisele Bündchen is able to use social platforms to highlight social, environmental, and animal causes. Although she has been supporting a variety of environmental causes, one could argue that many of the millions of people following her on Facebook, Twitter, and Instagram do not necessarily do so expecting to find such activism-related content. Through a quantitative and qualitative content analysis, we measured how people reacted to the activism content shared by her in 2017.

Celebrity Activism

Celebrities usually have limited or no institutional power, although they attract universal attention of society (Tsaliki et al., 2011). They can even alter the claims of a movement when they start to construct their legitimacy to speak for that movement (Meyer, 1995). Long before the World Wide Web, celebrities showed the world how they can use this power in social causes, as in Live Aid and Live 8 (Davis, 2010). Nowadays, with the popularity of the Internet, the World Wide Web, and social media, celebrities like Rihanna, Terry Crews, Lebron James, Taylor Swift, Chance the Rapper, Meghan Markle and Prince Harry, Beyoncé and Jay-Z, Jimmy Kimmel, and so on have a voice like they never had before to talk directly to their fans (Global Citizen, 2017), using social media to promote specific causes and to secure an active response from fan networks (Bennet, 2014).

Methodology

Content analysis can be applied to qualitative and quantitative data as an unobtrusive way to examine people's reactions, behavior, and communications (Babbie, 2010). Gisele published 1,138 posts on Facebook from 2012 to 2017. We chose the 2017 posts as our analysis sample in order to be able to manually analyze it and because those posts, being the most recent ones, better reflect her actual behavior in social media, and that of her followers, than the older ones.

Gisele Bündchen uses three social media platforms (Gisele Bündchen, 2018): Twitter (Twitter, 2018), Instagram (Instagram, 2018), and Facebook (Facebook, 2018). For this case study we chose Facebook due to the richness of the interactions, as fans are able to *like* and *follow* the fan page, *like*, *comment,* and *share* posts (which can be text, links, photos, and videos), and since 2016, users can react to a post using the new *Love, Haha, Wow, Sad*, and *Angry* buttons (Facebook Newsroom, 2018). As Gisele Bündchen uses a *fan page* and not a *personal profile*, it is also relatively easy to download and analyze all its data compared to the other two social media platforms.

We used a Python script (Nocodewebscraping, 2018) to download all Giselle Bündchen Facebook page data since her first post in March 2011 (Facebook, 2018). After downloading the data, we exported it to Microsoft Excel in order to analyze Gisele Bündchen's posts and the fans' reactions. After reading the 2017 posts, we noticed that when talking about activism, she basically talks about three subjects: environment, social cause, and animal rights. So we propose classifying the latent content of all her posts as follows: *environmental cause-related*; *social cause-related*; *animal cause-related*. In the next section we describe the sampling design.

Data gathering

We gathered 1,138 Facebook posts from March 10, 2011 to December 31, 2017. We filtered the posts from January 1, 2017 to December 31, 2017, finding a total of 90 posts. Due to the framework proposed in this case study, we coded those posts applying the classification we proposed in the Methodology session, considering the underlying meaning of each content item. We found that 31 out of 90 posts are related to activism. From those 31 posts, 25 are environmental cause-related, six are social cause-related, and just four are animal-related.

Data analysis

Among the top 10 posts with more reactions, none is environment/ social/animal-related. Actually, the first activist post appears only in the 16th position, as Figure 1 shows. On the other hand, among the top 10 posts with the least reactions, eight are activist-related. We also ranked all 2017 Gisele posts in order to analyze the frequency the activist posts appear among: 1) the most and the least commented posts; 2) the most and least shared posts; and 3) according to the type of reaction. The aim was to verify, in concrete terms through the manifest content, the reaction to activism posts in comparison to other themes.

Only 1 out of 10 most commented posts was environment-related, while 7 out of 10 among the least commented were activism-related. When we analyzed the most shared posts, we identified that 4 were activist posts. At the same time, 9 out of the 10 least shared posts were activist. We also considered the following reactions: *like*, *love*, *wow*, *haha*, and *sad*. Among the most liked posts none were activist posts, while 8 out of 10 posts with the least amount of *like* reaction were activist. Almost the same could be observed among the top 10 most and least loved posts: 1 out of 10 most loved was activist, and 8 out of 10 activist posts were among the least loved. From the top 10 posts with the most *Wow* reactions, two were activist, while 6 out of 10 posts with the least *Wow* reactions were activist. None of the top 10 posts with the most *Haha* reactions were activist, and among the top 10 with the least amount of *Haha*, eight were activist. Finally, the *Sad* reaction seems polarised. We found that 9 out of 10 posts with the most *Sad* reactions were activist, and 6 out of 10 posts among the least *Sad* reactions. We also noticed that *angry* was not a usual reaction among Gisele's followers. From the 90 posts analyzed, 82 had less than 10 *Angry* reactions and 29 had zero *Angry* reactions. Still, 5 out of 10 posts with the most *Angry* reactions were related to activism.

Classification	status_message	status_type	status_published	num_reactions
	Wonderful things come to those who work hard w	photo	06/02/17 12:43	182434
	Obrigada Ana Vilela por ter criado uma música tã	video	02/01/17 09:53	173453
	Bom dia! Game day! #superbowl #daddyslittlegirl	photo	05/02/17 09:13	155536
	We are ready! Let's go Tom Brady !! Let's go Pats	photo	05/02/17 15:07	133489
	Date night ❤ #Patriots super bowl ring ceremony	photo	09/06/17 18:25	125646
	Congratulations my love! @tom Tom Brady #gopa	photo	23/01/17 08:22	120966
	Love being your partner in the dance of life. Happy	photo	26/02/17 13:03	111816
	My date took me to the Maria Gadú concert last n	photo	02/04/17 11:27	94097
	Over 10 years ago I fell in love with you because o	photo	03/08/17 07:09	74620
		photo	02/05/17 15:02	72707
	Thank you my love Tom Brady! You are so sweet.	photo	04/05/17 08:49	70360
	What an honor to be projected on Empire State B	photo	20/04/17 11:33	69910
	Que saudades do verão! ☀ Missing summer!	photo	11/03/17 15:36	69484
	Pronta! #metgala	photo	01/05/17 20:48	67206
	#throwbackthursday Dona Florinda desde 1994 😘	photo	27/07/17 10:08	66948
	There is no bigger love that I have ever experience	photo	14/05/17 10:39	66061
Environment/social	Thank you Stella McCartney for my beautiful and s	photo	24/09/17 12:45	57379

Fig. 1. Posts with the most reactions.

Conclusion

During 2017 Gisele posted about activism 31% of the time. Most of those posts were about environmental causes and just a few about animal rights or social matters. Among the top 10 posts with more reactions, none was about activism. The top-rated activism-related post is ranked in the 16th position. On the other hand, among the 10 posts with the smallest number of reactions, eight were about activism. As Gisele is a Facebook user since 2011 and during this time won more than five million followers, we think her followers are more interested in her successful career, justifying their lack of interest in reacting to environmental causes. When we analyze the total comments per post, a similar phenomenon occurs: more comments on non-activist posts.

An interesting change happens when we analyze the total shares of a post and the total sad reactions. Among the 10 most shared posts, four are activism-related. Considering that Gisele posts about activism 31% of the time, the interest in sharing activism posts is slightly higher among the followers, although among the 10 least shared posts, just one is not about activism. When we analyze the sad reaction, 9 out of 10 "saddest" posts were about activism. We think this distortion may be related to the nature of the content, most of the time showing the harm mankind is doing to the environment.

We conclude that although Gisele Bündchen's followers are not primarily interested in her activist posts, she has a big impact in her activism as she is reaching a considerable number of people that probably were not looking for this kind of information when they started following her. Therefore, by engaging in activist causes and talking about this in 1 out of 3 posts, she endorses activist causes and reaches millions of followers, making a great impact on activism by inspiring and engaging people in activism.

As future work, we aim to extend this case study to other social media such as Instagram and Twitter. We also aim to compare Gisele Bündchen activism through social media to environmental/social/animal NGO's.

References

Babbie, E. (2010). *The Practice of Social Research*. Belmont: Wadsworth Cengage Learning.

Bennet, L. (2014). 'If We Stick Together We Can Do Anything':Lady Gaga Fandom, Philanthropy and Activism Thought Social Media. *Journal Celebrity Studies*, Vol 5, 2014, Issue 1-2

Davis, H. L. (2010). Feeding the World a Line?: Celebrity Activism and Ethical Consumer Practices From Live Aid to Product Red. *Nordic Journal of English Studies*, Vol 9, 2010, No 3

Eco-Age (2018, October 6). *The GCFA Award Winners 2017*. Retrieved from https://eco-age.com/news/gcfa-award-winners-2017

Facebook (2018, October 6). *Gisele Bündchen*. Retrieved from https://www.facebook.com/Gisele/

Facebook Newsroom (2018, October 6). *Reactions Now Available Globally*. Retrieved from https://newsroom.fb.com/news/2016/02/reactions-now-available-globally/

Forbes (2018, October 6). *The 20 Richest Women in Entertainment*. Retrieved from https://www.forbes.com/2007/01/17/richest-women-entertainment-tech-media-cz_lg_richwomen07_0118womenstars_lander.html#2703d5c9cd9c

Forbes Brasil (2018, October 6). *10 modelos mais bem pagas do mundo – 2017*. Retrieved from https://forbes.uol.com.br/listas/2017/11/10-modelos-mais-bem-pagas-de-2017/

Fortune (2018, October 6). *Gisele Bündchen Is Still the World's Highest-Paid Model*. Retrieved from http://fortune.com/2016/08/31/gisele-bundchen-highest-paid-model/

Gisele Bündchen (2018, October 6). *Bio*. Retrieved from http://giselebundchen.com

Global Citizen (2017, December 17). *These 9 Celebrity Activists Used Their Star Power for Good in 2017*. Retrieved from https://www.globalcitizen.org/en/content/celebrities-impact-top-2017-activism/

Instagram (2018, October 6). *gisele*. Retrieved from https://www.instagram.com/gisele/

International Green Awards (2018, October 6). *Best Green International Award – Gisele*. Retrieved from http://www.greenawards.com/green-awards-news/best-green-international-celebrity-award---gisele-bundchen

Meyer, David S. *The Challenge of Cultural Elites: Celebrities and Social Movements*.

Nocodewebscraping (2018, October 6). *How to Scrape Facebook Page Posts and Comments to Excel (with Python)*. Retrieved from https://nocodewebscraping.com/facebook-scraper/

Rolling Stone (2000, September 6). *Hot Girl: Giselle Bündchen*. Retrieved from https://www.rollingstone.com/culture/culture-news/hot-girl-gisele-bundchen-183901/

Tsaliki, L., Frangonikolopoulos, C. A., Huliaras, A. (2011). *Transnational Celebrity Activism in Global Politics: Changing the World?*. Intelect.

Twitter (2018, October 6). *Gisele Bündchen*. Retrieved from
  https://twitter.com/giseleofficial

United Nations Environment Programme (2018, October 6). *Gisele Bündchen.
  Supermodel, UN Environment Goodwill Ambassador – Global*. Retrieved from
  https://www.unenvironment.org/people/gisele-bundchen

Vanity Fair (2013, September 16). *There's something about Gisele*. Retrieved from
  https://www.vanityfair.com/news/2004/10/gisele-bundchen-fashion-film-debut

Voguepedia (2018, October 6). *Gisele Bündchen*. Retrieved from WebArchive
  https://web.archive.org/web/20140331204652/http://www.vogue.com/voguepedia/
  Gisele_Bundchen

The Ethical Beauty of Poverty: The Empowerment of Bibi Russell's Celebrity to Transform Traditional Concepts of Glamour

Luis Fernando Romo

Abstract. In the twentieth century, the machinery of Hollywood's Golden Age transformed glamour into a magnetic impulse endorsed by the film stars. Later, during the 1980s and 1990s, glamour and fashion became increasingly intertwined through ritualized fashion catwalks, forging a new rhetoric of glamour around the celebrity supermodel. Thus, the glamor and celebrity increased the bond with audiences by conveying values such as beauty, luxury, and lifestyle. Bibi Russell, a respected Bangladeshi supermodel, strutted the runways for a variety of luxury brands such as Valentino and Saint Laurent, and featured in major campaigns for Rolls Royce and Harper's Bazaar. Today, Bibi is a renowned fashion designer, utilizing the celebrity capital of her name as a vehicle to promote local Bangladeshi artisans. This paper investigates the under-recognized nexus of (ethical) beauty and poverty, through ethically sustainable collections and ecological consciousness to create new conceptualizations of glamour.

Keywords: Bangladesh, Bibi Russell, ethical beauty, glamour, poverty.

Introduction

There has been very little academic work that analytically investigates the bonds among glamour, ethics, fashion, beauty and, most importantly, poverty. It can be remarked what Lamrad & Hanlon (2014) admit regarding the scarcity of further theoretical investigations into Fashion for Development and Ethics. In addition, special attention should be given to two scholars. Gundle reveals that "the realm of glamour is a universe inhabited by the very wealthy, the talented, the beautiful, the famous, and the lucky" (2008, p. 3) and Prendergast, 1992, cited in Douglas (2009), affirms that in the sphere of glamour "the poor are excluded, and the spectacle and the pleasures it promises is a matter of class". (p. 48)

This paper aims to demonstrate two hypotheses: firstly, that glamour can perform new definitions according to the '(aesth)ethics' of Bibi Russell's fashion designs; and, secondly, beauty and glamour may be associated with poverty creating a collective identity according to Bangladeshi ethical codes.

What is glamour? Many scholars have attempted to define fame, celebrity and rumor, topics usually associated with glamour, without ever truly achieving a conclusive description. Since its appearance as a modern idea in English texts at the beginning of the nineteenth century[1], glamour still entails polyhedral definitions. Gundle (2008, p. 4) defines it as "a weapon and a protective coating, a screen on which an exterior personality can be built to deceive, delight, and bewitch", and Postrel affirms that is "an illusion which is known to be false but felt to be true" (2013, p. 44).

Through the evolution of its conceptualization, glamour has been typically associated with celebrities that belonged to an aristocratic environment (Gundle & Castelli, 2006; Gundle, 2008). Nevertheless, the commodification of everyday life, the proliferation of the modern bourgeoise sphere along with the development of photography and cinematography democratized glamour to include the lower social strata (Rojek, 2001; Williamson, 2016). With regard to this, from 1907, Hollywood started to create what deCordova (2001) called "picture personalities[2]," who were the antecedents for the emergence of the star. (Walker, 1970; McDonald, 2000).

As an ethereal and elusive concept (Reynolds, 2014), glamour may be considered a form of communication and persuasion for social cohesion and longing. In order for this to happen, from the nineteenth century glamour brought together a whole series of features that not only referred to the individual, but also to their environment (Gundle, 2008, Dyhouse, 2010). Features such as wealth, sophistication, refinement, lifestyle, beauty, mystery, visibility, influence, the power of attraction, and scandal. In this way, the Veblen good was increased to a superlative degree by the extravagant consumption of an ostentatious lifestyle (Lowenthal, 2006) due to elements that are part of the visual culture: cosmetics, clothes, exquisite garments, jewelry, and refined decoration.

In the process of disseminating the image of the film stars as manufactured commodities (Dyer, 2004; Driessens, 2014), photographers were one of the essential "cultural intermediaries" (Redmond, 2014). The same would happen in photography in the fashion world. The black and white stars' studio portraits of Steichen, Hurrell, and Beaton were the most prominent assets to '(re)generate' the idea of modern glamour (Gundle, 2008; Slide, 2010; Postrel, 2013; Reynolds, 2014).

Visual strategies embodied the new perception of glamour. The result was a scenario printed in black and white gelatin silver where the dominance were the close-ups of the stars with sparkling contrasts, sharp focus, vaporous

[1] Sir Walter Scott introduced the word glamour in The Lay of the Last Minstrel in 1805.

[2] First film actors and actresses treated as celebrities.

murkiness, and seductive poses (Reynolds, 2014; Keating, 2017). Their technique influenced their 'heirs' Herb Ritts, Patrick Demarchelier and Mario Testino, who reinforced the imaginary of glamour due to the publicized top model phenomenon which emerged from the eighties and nineties. The new "Olympiens" (Morin, 1963) were supermodels Bibi Russell, Jerry Hall, Janice Dickinson, and Cindy Crawford, who were declared the new faces of beauty having acquired part of the (beauty) mystique of the movie stars. It was the rebirth of glamour.

For instance, many professionals in the industry and fans alike felt Claudia Schiffer looked like the French actress Brigitte Bardot. Over the course of time, the meaning and perception of glamour has been transformed in order to achieve social, economic, and cultural aims. Undoubtedly, the purpose of ex-top model-turned-fashion designer Bibi Russell is to associate glamour to beauty, poverty, ethically sustainable collections, and ecological ideals.

From the principle of African society, 'You are because we are' to help the community and the concept of the 'enough economy' of Buddhism, it can be said that Bibi Russell has re-envisioned glamour as a social equilibrium entity in which the simple things of life are the authentic luxury. The heritage, the respect, the raw materials, the (in)tangible poverty, and the facilitation of social and occupational integration are part of the new meaning of the ethical cost of beauty through social impoverishment. Thus, Bibi Russell utilizes her name as a vehicle for the visibility of the work of local Bangladeshi weavers and artisans.

Bibi Russell, a 'Model' as an Etrepreneur

As a UNESCO Goodwill Ambassador, Bibi Russell symbolizes the handicraft industry around the world. She was born in Chattogram, Bangladesh, in 1950. She traveled to England where she graduated from the prestigious London College of Fashion in 1975. After that, she became one of the best-known models of the seventies and eighties, having appeared on the covers and pages of Harper's Bazaar, Vogue, and Marie Claire; modeling for prestigious labels such as Valentino, Armani, and Saint Laurent; and campaigning for such luxury brands as Rolls Royce and Jaguar. At that time, Bibi Russell, Jerry Hall, and Zara Abdulmajid, better known as Iman, were the most sought-after top models.

Figure 1. Bibi Russell was appointed UNESCO Artist for Peace in 1999.

Nevertheless, despite the world of glamour and luxury lifestyle in which Bibi was immersed, she decided to return to her roots in 1994, and one year later, she founded Bibi Productions, Fashion for Development. Muhammad Yunus, the founder of the Grameen Bank, helped her to develop her company through microcredits and microfinance. Since then, Russell has epitomized the new concept of green glamour, which encompasses specific features. Her collections are handmade designs made in the traditional way of weaving cotton, natural dyes, and resources, vibrant colors, with no synthetic fabrics as well as ethical development and ecological thinking in order to preserve the traditional crafts and textiles. Thus, tradition is preserved through the generations.

Changing the Glamour Mystique

Being away from the paraphernalia of the coveted red carpets, Bibi Russell has reimagined glamour by creating a discourse of poverty. As Lamrad & Hanlon (2014) claim, "Fashion for Development products are constituted of a unique set of signals, or codes, that support symbolic frameworks geared toward notions of poverty alleviation." (p. 614) If traditional glamour is partly linked to wealth, mystery, extravagant jewels, lavish designs, scandal, and black and white photography, Bibi has been creating a new narrative that reconstructs and complements the glamour mystique's symbolic narrative. Despite being an ethical fashion icon, Bibi Russell has preserved some of the attributes of traditional glamour as fashion, beauty, lifestyle, visibility, and power of attraction.

The meaning and visual treatment of these elements alongside the innate qualities of the designer -her charisma, reputation, credibility, and talent- embody an "economic, cultural and social capital" (Bourdieu, 2011) which can be transformed into money, preservation of the tradition, and influence in the next generation.

As said in the introduction, glamour is not only about the individual but also about the environment. It is a capitalist economy versus impoverished countries. Due to Bibi's 'celebrity capital' defined as an "accumulated media visibility through recurrent media representations" (Driessens, 2013, p. 13), Bibi has seen beauty beyond poverty and has always been conscious that glamour is ephemeral and can be reconceptualized it in her collections. Thus, tradition is preserved throughout the generations.

The Hidden 'Luxury' of Poverty

Poverty has always been forgotten. Nevertheless, Bibi Russell saw in it a diamond in the rough. After more than two decades, she has been polishing poverty to make it into a precious commodity. "My work is not to show the misery, but to show the world the beauty which lies in poverty". (B. Russell, personal communication, June 27, 2018)

Although Bangladesh is one of the most impoverished countries in the world, the specificity and quality of its handmade textiles have been recognized as being amongst the most delicate fabrics on the planet for many centuries. In this instance, UNESCO described the first fibers in her collections as refined silks, hand-woven muslin, and a wide range of Khadi.

By utilizing high-quality fibers and natural sources such as water hyacinth, coconut shells, and terracotta (Rahman, 2013), Bibi has created a sustainable label whose core is to preserve the tradition of Bangladeshi artisans and weavers. The craftspeople observe and listen to achieve a natural inspiration to make significant economic and social development to nurture education, to create employment, and eradicate poverty. It is vital to understand and care about what is theirs and forge an industry so that the next generation can have a good education and health. Bibi is visually marked as peculiar because she mixes the past and the present in her collections. Thus, tradition is preserved through the generations.

Figure 2. In her collections, Bibi Russell works to develop traditional textiles and handicrafts. © Bibi Russell Productions

Ethics Applied in Beauty

Bibi is branding her people considering poverty as a medium to achieve ethical values away from materialism and opulence, which are the main traits of occidental fashion. Like Bibi Russell's company, other designers and organizations such as the Rwandan prêt-à-porter jewelry designer Eden Diodati, the Cameroonian fashion designer Imane Ayissi or the textile social economy concept of Arropa in Spain are based in the social economy to develop co-responsibility, respect, fair business relationships, and trust. (Gardetti & Delgado, 2018)

Ethics is the pillar of her environmentally friendly and hand-made collections because she believes that fashion can be used for social, economic development and a positive movement. Bibi enables the weavers and the craftspeople to enhance their opportunities to achieve education, human dignity, and the preservation of their traditions.

Figure 3. The fashion designer wants to preserve the heritage of Bangladesh, foster creativity, provide employment, and contribute towards the eradication of poverty. © Bibi Russell Productions

Bibi Russell has served as an intermediary between the real and the imaginary. Hence, her ideas and the workforce of the craftspeople altogether create a collective identity with shared social values. As Bibi says:

> Now I am wearing glasses, in my eyes, my smile, my mental satisfaction, everything that is the ethical beauty what I see in poverty. You see the joy, the happiness, the confidence on these people you know which I went to transform in my creation because they are the one sitting there, waiting for people to respect the human dignity. Just you have to walk around you can see everywhere the ethical beauty of poverty. (B. Russell, personal communication, June 27, 2018)

In this sense, Bibi Russell has developed the ethic of beauty of poverty.

Conclusion

This case study demonstrates that through her collections, Bibi Russell has been capable of reformulating the idea of glamour in an environment in which poverty is the common denominator. Bibi's designs are a vivid example of the transformation of the traditional concept of glamour into a new narrative in which exquisite natural fabrics are the primary source of beauty. Bibi Russell is bridging gaps between the industry of fashion and traditional craftspeople, in order to develop sustainable enterprises. Cultural diversity boosts sustainable crafts and the preservation of heritage. Through Bibi Russell Productions, the quality of life for the craftspeople has improved dramatically due to Bibi Russell's moral commitment to the environment, the promotion of their handmade textile traditions, and the creation of employment opportunities. Ethics is the pedestal on which this Bangladeshi fashion designer has built a sustainable empire.

References

Bourdieu, P. (2011). The forms of capital (1986). *Cultural theory: An anthology, 1,* 81-93.

DeCordova, R. (2001). *Picture personalities: the emergence of the star system in America.* Illinois (US): University of Illinois Press.

Douglas, G. (2009). What is Glamour? The Production & Consumption of a Working Aesthetic. *MU-DOT: The Magazine for Urban Documentation, Opinion and Theory,* (2)44.

Driessens, O. (2014). Theorizing celebrity cultures: Thickenings of media cultures and the role of cultural (working) memory. *Communications, 39*(2). doi:10.1515/commun-2014-0008.

Dyer, R. (2004). *Heavenly bodies. Film stars and society.* New York: Routledge.

Dyhouse, C. (2010). *Glamour: Women, History, Feminism.* London & New York: Zed Books.

Gardetti, M.Á., & Delgado Luque, M. L. (2018). *Vestir un mundo sostenible: La moda de ser humanos en una industria polémica.* Buenos Aires: LID Editorial Empresarial, S.R.L.

Gundle, S., & Castelli, C. (2006). *The glamour system.* New York: Palgrave Macmillan.

Gundle, S. (2008). *Glamour: a history.* New York: Oxford University Press.

Keating, P. (2017). Artifice and Atmosphere: The Visual Culture of Hollywood Glamour Photography, 1930–1935. *Film History, 29*(3), 105-135.

Lamrad, N., & Hanlon, M. (2014). Untangling fashion for development. *Fashion Theory, 18*(5), 601-631.

Lowenthal, L. (2006). The Triumph of Mass Idols. In P. D. Marshall (Ed.), *The Celebrity Culture Reader* (pp. 124-152). New York & Oxon (UK): Routledge.

McDonald, P. (2000). *The star system: Hollywood's production of popular identities.* London & New York: Wallflower Press.

Morin, V. (1963). Les Olympiens. In: *Communications*, 2, 1963. pp. 105-121. doi: https://doi.org/10.3406/comm.1963.949.

Postrel, V. (2013). *The power of glamour: Longing and the art of visual persuasion.* New York: Simon and Schuster.

Rahman, F. S. (2013). Fashion technology park Hatijheel (Thesis Bachelor in Architecture). BRAC University, Dhaka, Bangladesh. (Retrieved from http://dspace.bracu.ac.bd/xmlui/handle/10361/3141).

Redmond, S. (2014). *Celebrity and the Media.* London & New York: Palgrave Macmillan.

Reynolds, A. (2014). Edward Steichen and Hollywood Glamour (Master's Thesis). Available from https://uknowledge.uky.edu/art_etds/9.

Rojek, C. (2004). *Celebrity.* London: Reaktion Books.

Slide, A. (2010). *Inside the Hollywood Fan Magazine: A History of Star Makers, Fabricators, and Gossip Mongers.* Mississippi (US): Univ. Press of Mississippi.

Thomas, D. (2007). *Deluxe: How luxury lost its luster.* New York: Penguin Books.

Walker, A. (1970). *Stardom: The Hollywood phenomenon.* New York: Stein and Day.

Williamson, M. (2016). *Celebrity: Capitalism and the making of fame.* Cambridge (UK): Polity Press.

Echoes of Ecofeminism: The Resonance of Glamour Labor and (Somatic) Ethics in Contemporary Literature

Birte Fritsch and Patrick Nogly

Abstract. Regarding Frédéric Beigbeders novel *Au secours pardon* (2007), this chapter emphasizes the social and socio-political discourse on fashion, fashion industry, and physical *glamour labour* (Wissinger, 2015) as reflected in contemporary literary production in the Western hemisphere. Focusing on an elaborate, satirical and, therefore, highly abstract and artificial text rather than taking into account the often addressed *Chick Lit* texts, we want to highlight the productive interconnection between high culture and haute couture, and their intertwined discursive potentials. *Au secours pardon* discusses actual matters of *feminism* and *gender* – as the commodification of women in the fashion industry as depicted in this novel is 'literally' still virulently ongoing – and thereby arises questions of *somatic ethic(s)* (Rose, 2007) and the *biopolitics of beauty* (Zylinska, 2007). We would like to stress the matters of consumption and the inherent need of transformation of self in terms of *Ecofeminism*: the role women are to take in and outside the *fashion sphere* which is evidently related to the (human) domination and exploitation of nature in the Anthropocene (Zabinski, 1997). Analyzing the Beigbederian novel through the queries postured by critical *ecofeminism* (Antón Fernández, 2017), we want to point out how aesthetic artefacts have a potential influence on the discourse 'shaping' the future of beauty industry.

Keywords: ecofeminism, somatic ethics, glamour labor, Frédéric Beigbeder.

Introduction

Following the *#MeToo* movement, the discussion on the female role in (the business of) acting, showing, and representing – the female persona in representing womanhood in different domains of an artificial public sphere – constantly reminds us (1) that women overall still are not treated equally and (2) of the abuse of women. The inequality is ongoing within and beyond this specific field and it is ostensibly acknowledged without any further complaint from a majority of the society.

In this chapter, we want to reflect upon the discursive potentials of literary texts in bringing into focus the exploitation of female protagonists, both in the fictional aesthetic artifact and its factual critical reception (reader-response), and the criteria provided by (feminist) ethical approaches presented hereafter.

Ecofeminism(s) and Other Ethical Approaches to the not so Beautiful Sphere of the Beauty Industry

Ecofeminism(s)

First coined in 1974 by the French feminist Françoise d'Eaubonne[1] and building on the concepts of 2nd wave Feminism, the term ecofeminism depicts the interconnection between the domination of nature and the inferiorization of women – alluding to the 'inherent' connection of women and nature. This thus not uncomplicated relation (in)directly emphasizes the naturalization of women and the commodification, destruction, and oppression of both women and nature.

As a part of environmental ethics, ecofeminism is constantly questioning political and personal behavioral practices. It also depicts Western dualisms as dominant at all times and interconnected to relations of power and suppression. Dichotomies such as technology and nature, reason and emotion, and mind and body have not only defined Western intellectual discourses since antiquity, but they form the basis of a differentiating system in which structures of male superiority are likely to be linked to reason and thinking, while female qualities are attributed to nature and emotion as they literally incorporate physical aspects of fertility: in menstruating, becoming pregnant, carrying children, breast-feeding etc. – women allegedly embody their sensual 'bodyness'.

Despite the above-mentioned aspects of gender binaries, contemporary ecofeminism(s) and other critical bases also take into consideration forms of dominance and suppression with an emphasis on further intersectional aspects such as race and class. Ecofeminism can thereby be defined as a

> [V]alue system, a social movement, and a practice [...] [which] also offers a political analysis that explores the links between androcentrism and environmental destruction. It is an "awareness" that begins with the realization that the exploitation of nature is intimately linked to Western man's attitude toward women and tribal cultures. (Birkeland 1993: 8)

Somatic Ethic(s)

In using an ecofeminist approach, we can start identifying existing power structures that commodify the female body in Western capitalist systems of glamour and shift its imbalance towards representing female bodies in a more

---

[1] First mentioned in: Françoise d'Eaubonne (1974): *Le féminisme ou la mort.*

ethical manner. To this end, Nicolas Rose's concept of the 'somatic ethic' is useful to consider in productions of ethical glamour, fashion, and style:

> Human beings identify and interpret much of their unease in terms of the health, vitality, and morbidity of their bodies; they judge and act upon their soma in their attempts to make themselves not just physically better but also to make themselves better persons. This is what I call a 'somatic ethic' (Rose 2007: 3).

Somatic ethics, in Nicolas Rose's sense, are based on the active act of shaping the private self and, by this means, on the biopoetics of the modern life itself: biomedicine, power and sustainability, self-optimization, and biocapital. These contemporary, rather 'trendy' concepts of an ideal life are themselves likewise based on the link between mind and body, *soma* and *ratio*, as shown in the Western dualisms above. Becoming a better person, optimizing one's life, reaching the state of health and happiness – *mens sana in corpore sane* – are nowadays closely related to a strict *somatism*. The political and ethical implications and openings made possible by this fetishization of corporeality as the 'embodied life' are to be witnessed in the contemporary social and socioeconomical debates (e.g., in US politics), as well as in commonplace content or comments on social media.

From an ecofeminist perspective, the internalization of this kind of normalizing judgment leads to new, superficial, strictly visible and thereby glaring dualisms such as underweight vs. obese that is equated with beautiful vs. ugly, and so on. Unfortunately, and this should not be ignored, those strictly superficial and subjectively sustained norms and principles are gaining acceptance and more and more relevance in our ethic value system—as well as in the capitalist value chain that needs to be critically explored and articulated in feminist productions and representations of ethical glamour, fashion, and style.

Biopolitics of Beauty

In her "critical-creative work of bioethics",[2] Joanna Zylinska further aims:

> [T]o shift the parameters of the conventional bioethical debate - from an individualistic problem-based moral paradigm [...] to a broader political context in which individual decisions are always involved in complex relations of power, economy, and ideology. This non-normative ethics of inevitable enhancement can [...] be taken as a pre-condition of

---

[2] Zylinska (2012:219)

'responsible biopolitics'[…] [and] must also become – if need be – the bad conscience of dominant bioethics. (Zylinska 2010: 159)

In her works, Zylinska focuses mainly on media and communication. She describes that the biopolitical logic of modernity can be linked to the concepts mentioned above. As she defines the actual Western norm of the constant need for optimization – of bodies and life, of self and others – she also takes into consideration concepts of *otherness* and *alterity*.

Philosophical approaches to bioethics might lead to a differentiated view on cultivation and domestication of a female still being referred to as inferior. The increasing degree of 'life management' in our Western society reinforces and impels the ongoing battle of the sexes. In the field of the fashion industry, those effect mechanisms are driven by the power of capitalist economics, an interrelationship not mentioned so far but needs to be re-examined in practices of glamour and style.

Ecofeminisim(s) and the Fashion Sphere

As women are still in many ways oppressed by men and a somatic self-optimization has become one of the main patterns of a consumption-oriented Western society, the fashion industry might be a prime example of this paradigm. In objectifying the female body as a trading good, a display(ed) dummy, the commodified female *soma* gains its attributed value from a system governed by (male) power structures, which suppresses female empowerment and intellectuality. Newer forms of *persona branding* might offer a way out of this dilemma in productions and representation of ethical glamour, fashion, and style.

The Business of Aesthetic Representation Represented in the Aesthetic Artefact

In dealing with the artifacts in the literary and artistic field (Bourdieu 1992), the discursive potentials of the depicted social and socioeconomic aspects and threats of contemporary glamour labor are intertwined with the reader's construction of meaning, as the following close reading of Beigbeder's novel, *Au secours pardon* shall illustrate.

To offer women living in precarious situations an opportunity to escape their social environments and thus to accomplish their dreams sounds like a rather altruistic gesture, something worthy of being held in high regard. What Frédéric Beigbeder's novel *Au secours pardon* shows us, through the eye of the figure Octave, the truth behind those seemingly altruistic gestures and the abysses that opens up behind the alleged perfection of fashion and cosmetic industries.

The novel is about a man in his 40s who works as a model scout in Russia. His job is to find the perfect face to represent L'Idéal, the leading cosmetic company (there is an unambiguous allusion to the brand L'Oréal…). The main character, Octave, gives us an insight of what it means to be a model scout, to work within the cosmetic and fashion industries, on the one hand, and what it is like to be, as a man, a representative of a world ruled by men, on the other. The novel identifies a world in which women are being objectified and treated as mere products to be sold as cheap as possible; a world full of drugs, violence, and sex in which women are nothing but a mannequin and a soma, whose value is determined by a masculine sense of beauty.

Octave presents this world in a quite critical manner, at least until he admits to being a contributor in it and playing the game. Hence, his approach is *grosso modo* to seduce, to convince, to dominate, and to abuse women—a price women are supposed to pay in order to fulfill their dreams. In the novel, sexual assault, literally and metaphorically, is the easiest way to figure out whether a woman is worth being promoted or not. The perfect woman, obviously and in the first place, must be young; the younger she is, the more likely she will be accepted and get the chance of becoming a model. This is exactly what Octave's first impression was: the younger a model is, the more lucrative and desirable she becomes.

> Au début j'avais l'impression d'être le seul à m'inquiéter de voir toute une industrie devenir pédophile. Comme mes confrères semblaient tous trouver la situation normale, je cessai bientôt de m'en préoccuper. Et c'est ainsi que j'ai travaillé tranquillement à donner aux hommes du monde entier l'envie de coucher avec des enfants. (Beigbeder 2007: 36)[3]

If we now link the protagonist's experience to what previously was defined as ecofeminism, we see that Beigbeder, through the figure Octave, points out how women are transformed and reduced to somewhat like a head of cattle ready to be hunted. The scouts or model hunters chase and catch women, degrading them to animalized objects, appraised as merchandise of a certain commercial value set by men, of course. "Je faisais des classements de filles, des hitparades physiques, des listes de visages" (Beigbeder 2007: 40)[4], Octave sums up. A

---

[3] At first, I felt like I was the only one to worry about seeing a whole industry become paedophile. As my colleagues all seemed to consider it a normal situation, I soon stopped fretting about it. And so I worked on quietly to give men all around the world the urge to sleep with minors.

[4] I made classifications of girls, physical chart, lists of faces.

little later he goes into greater detail pointing out that "je devais aborder la beauté afin de la saborder. Pour cela, il fallait toujours commencer par convaincre la fille de ma probité, puis ensuite faire miroitier les roubles devant ses parents." (Beigbeder 2007: 81)[5]

Furthermore, while speaking about searching for a Chechen woman, Octave affirms that there is, in that world, also a lot of racism. In this sense, the selection of women turns out to be at the same time a rather political decision, another essential factor that determines whether a woman is chosen or not. Besides their beauty and youth, their ethnic backgrounds become a relevant component. What is considered beautiful, what represents the man-made ideal of beauty, is finally a political and racist decision, the result of which is that race and racism are a constitutive part of our ideal of beauty.

Lastly, a few words must be said regarding the products these women are to represent. There are, in fact, connections to other economic sectors; that is to say that the products offered by L'Idéal, for example, are related to the oil industry controlled by Russian oligarchs. These product endorsements allow us to link the exploitation of nature directly to that of women, a link that can be taken as an example for other products within the cosmetic industry, in general, that require testing on animals, the killing of living organisms, and so on and so forth. Ultimately, there is, at least so it seems, almost no difference between the exploitation of nature as seen on animals and plants, and that of women in fashion and cosmetic industries. As we argued earlier in this article, the connection between women and nature is one of the core elements of early ecofeminism. Although there is no explicit link between the exploitation of women and that of nature can be found in Beigbeder's novel, other novels like Margaret Atwood's *Surfacing* could be related directly to what Ortner, following the argumentation of de Beauvoir, would call the "universal devaluation of women" (Ortner 1972: 7) and postulate that "woman is seen as 'closer to nature'"(Ortner 1972: 24). What relates nature to women in the novel is the way in which both spheres are exploited in order to benefit hierarchical systems represented by the oligarchic system, on the one hand, and the fashion and cosmetic industries, on the other. Given the fact that both systems are, in a certain sense, intertwined reinforces this point as can be seen in the following statement of Octave: "L'Idéal préparait le lancement d'une nouvelle molécule antivieillissement produite par Oilneft, le groupe dirigé par mon pote Serguëi

---

[5] I had to approach beauty in order to scuttle it. For that, it was always necessary to start by convincing the girl of my integrity, then to make the roubles shine in front of her parents.

l'oligarque" (Beigbeder 2007: 83)[6]. L'Idéal and Oilneft collaborate and, if women are being objectified and exploited in order to become a model representing the products of L'Idéal, natural resources are being exploited in order to provide the basic material to create and present the newest cosmetic products. There could be a lot more said about the relation found between the exploitation of nature and that of women, a desideratum for further research,

Conclusion: High Culture and Haute Couture

Beigbeder's novel, as well as other (literary) contributions in high and pop culture, reflects on the vibrantly, ongoing suppression of female equality and individuality for the (economic) benefit of a hierarchic system governed by straight white masculinity.

Within the novel, "L'Idéal" as a name, a signifier, represents all of the above said in itself: Beigbeder drew a vivid and thereby utterly realist picture of the beauty industry and the ongoing exploitation of women in the 21st century driven by the idealization of supra-individual somatic traits.

In shaping the discourse on glamour labor, an aesthetic artifact inherits the potential to shift the place of discussion from the sociological field into the individual, intimate sphere of reader-response. Further readings could lead to questions of *art engagé,* the role of the author – as in this case, Beigbeder has been an agent in both fields: the art and entertainment industries.

References

Antón Fernández, E. (2017). Claves ecofeministas para el análisis literario, *GénEros*, Vol: 24, N° 21.

Ash, J. and Wilson E. (eds.) (1992). *Chic Thrills: A Fashion Reader*. Berkeley: University of California Press.

Beigbeder, F. (2007). *Au secours pardon*. Paris: Grasset.

Bourdieu, P. (1992). *Les règles de l'art: genèse et structure du champ littéraire*. Paris: Seuil.

Butler, J. (1990). *Gender Trouble: Feminism and the Subversion of Identity*. New York: Routledge.

de Beauvoir, S. (1952). *The Second Sex*. (Translated by H.M. Parshley). New York: Knopf.

---

[6] L'Idéal prepared the launch of a new anti-aging molecule produced by Oilneft, the group directed by my friend Sergej the oligarch.

d'Eaubonne, F. (1974). *Le féminisme ou la mort*. Paris: Horay.

Gaard, G. (1997). Toward a Queer Ecofeminism, *Hypatia*, 12(1).

Lamontagne, A. (1998). Métatextualité postmodeme: de la fiction à la critique, *Études littéraires,* 30(3), 61-76.

Mears, A. (2011). *Pricing Beauty: The Making of a Fashion Model.* Los Angeles: University of California Press.

Neff, G., Wissinger, E. and Zukin, S. (2005). Entrepreneurial Labor among Cultural Producers: 'Cool' Jobs in 'Hot' Industries, *Social Semiotics,* 15(3), 307–334.

Ortner, S. B. (1972). Is Female to Male as Nature Is to Culture?, *Feminist Studies,* 1(2), 5-31.

Rose, N. (2006). *The Politics of Life Itself: Biomedicine, Power, and Subjectivity in the 21st Century.* Princeton: Princeton University Press.

Rose, N. (2007). Molecular Biopolitics, Somatic Ethics and the Spirit of Biocapital, *Social Theory and Health* N° 5.

van Wesemael, S. (2011). *Le roman transgressif contemporain: de Bret Easton Ellis à Michel Houellebecq,* Paris: L' Harmattan.

Wissinger, E. A. (2015). *This Year's Model: Fashion, Media, and the Making of Glamour.* New York: New York University Press.

Zabinski, C. (1997). Scientific Ecology and Ecological Feminism, in Karen J. Warren (ed.): *Ecofeminism: Women, Culture, Nature.* Bloomington and Indianapolis: Indiana University Press, pp. 314-325.

Zylinska, J. (2007). Of Swans and Ugly Ducklings: Bioethics between Humans, Animals, and Machines, *Configurations* 15(2), 125–150.

Joanna Z. (2012). Bioethics Otherwise, or, How to Live with Machines, Humans, and Other Animals, in Tom Cohen (ed.) *Telemorphosis: Theory in the Era of Climate Change*, v. 1. Open Humanities Press, pp. 211-230.

From Journalism to Fashion Activism: Refashioning Stories for Social Change - Interview with Kabir Bedi

Samita Nandy

Today celebrity activists and fashion models are accomplishing what most journalism schools cannot. While this statement is rooted in controversy, influencers and activists have come to rely on storytelling, both literally and visually, to help their fans spark social change.

This is what international actor and Oscar-voting member Kabir Bedi indicates in his radical views of journalism education. He also expresses his opinion on the critical state of the tabloid press — especially when it comes to violence, fake news, and scandals.

'The real scandal is not who slept with who,' explains the Sandokan star at the Mumbai Soho House in India. 'The real scandal is when that building collapsed in Bangladesh, and it shows the extent of exploitation in the fashion world — how many big names are involved and how many of those names have become responsive today as a result of that accident and loss of life.'

The rhetorical question in #WhoMadeMyClothes is gaining a valid response beyond tabloid journalism in the fashion revolution.

In this regard, Bedi believes there is an entire movement taking place, and he is certain it will continue to pick up steam. It has become increasingly clear that public figures have been condemned for not challenging the status quo — for perpetuating the embodiment of normative identity, and for circulating gender myths. But those who criticize the unachievable standards of beauty models and celebrities bring can do so much more than simply retweet a trending hashtag.

Rather, they can use autoethnographic learning tools and share stories of the Gandhian change they wish to inspire.

Yet, while victims in the post-Weinstein era need not be excluded from class-based responses to the star-studded #MeToo movement, such is far too often the plight of the oppressed. Many victims' use of #MeToo in Hollywood and Bollywood celebrity culture just is not enough.

And despite the prominence of higher education and online news, there are similar observations involving 'lookism' in the discrimination of race, class, and species, as well as other marginalized categories.

This illustrates that words can fail. Moreover, while rationality has opened the door for progressive thinking, it has also enabled greater categorization and discrimination. Nonetheless, activists are using visual storytelling to help others bring positive change. They are refashioning stories, and inspiring fans, students, and scholars in the process.

But how?

As the 7th Centre for Media and Celebrity Studies (CMCS) conference in Lisbon demonstrated, models, actors, authors, academics, and athletes have taken to stylizing their profile pictures and building their personal brands through visual and literary expressions of fashion. When it comes to choosing between being a storywriter or a storyteller, taking action via aesthetic means and becoming a citizen journalist are conscious decisions we must make.

From my perspective, as an author and model without agency representation, I appropriated and employed sustainable fashion for my cruelty-free brown skin. This, I found, allowed me to navigate the cultural spaces where celebrities are represented and mediated in fandom. There is no single-issue cause here, as the roots of oppression overlap.

Accordingly, the speciesism and sexism that once rendered me invisible — all for the sake of family honour — could have been addressed with the visual representation I offer now. That is what it means to be excluded.

Fortunately, today expressions of fashion are playing a key role in the publicity and promotion of many public figures' ethical brands. I've learned this both in my own experience and by observing other activists in their effort to spark transformation.

This brings us to an essential question: can students and fans refashion stories and normalize some of the much-needed democratic practices in celebrity activism, journalism, and academic studies involving popular culture? If not, what are the ethical issues at play in tabloid journalism that must be addressed at the societal level?

The interview below explores the answers to these questions and others like them. Readers will find that Kabir Bedi draws on his activism experience in Hollywood and Bollywood, and offers deep insights into the dichotomy of the tabloid press.

Kabir Bedi: Tabloid journalism, by its very nature, will want to seize sensational stories. It needs headlines, so whatever is the most sensational aspect of the story, that's what will be highlighted. As far as fandom goes, fans want any and all information — whether it is authentic or from tabloid or whatever — they are just hungry for information.

The ethical issue that arises — what is real and what is not, what is valid and what is not, what is true and what is not — that is not an easy thing to sort out because there is no source by which you can say that I will go and check out what the truth of the matter is.

There are sites celebrities have on themselves — they have a certain amount of information. They will naturally give the best information about themselves — they won't give the worst. Therefore, one has to reach out to various levels of social media to try and balance what is true and what is not true, especially when it comes to what appears in the tabloids.

News no longer filters down from the top — it's not like what we have had from the New York Times, the Washington Post, and CNN — and everything goes down to the bottom of the pyramid. Today bottom of the pyramid is talking to each other — they have all kinds of other sources of information. No matter what your hobby is, what your interest is — you will always find some group on the Internet that you will relate to, that is interested in things you are interested in — whether it is information about a star, information about fans – these groups may help you to sift some of the weed from the chaff but not always. It is an 'imperfect science,' and it will always remain that.

Samita Nandy: Do you think that journalism educators should encourage their students and overall readers to access websites or any sort of platform that celebrities and celebrity activists maintain themselves for an authentic voice?

Kabir Bedi: Journalism educators should be aware of the reach and form of social media because it's not just the Facebooks, Twitters and Instagrams as the only source of information. You can get an enormous amount of information from Youtube, Wikipedia, and sites that are created by the celebrities themselves.

You can get an enormous amount of information from mainstream press. Journalism educators' biggest job is to train their students in the sheer number of sources of information that exist today for getting information and from that information, how to distill what is closest to the truth because there are no shortcuts to that.

When there are multiple voices singing, you have to figure out which are the right tones.

There are so many aspects to stories today.

And there is so much PR spin that comes in as well because today journalists aren't really doing the 'beat' — looking for stories. They are sitting in offices and stories are being given to them pre-packaged stories by PR agencies with glossy photos and brilliant write-ups all ready made. So the incentive for them to go out and hunt for the truth is greatly reduced — they have only a certain number of columns to fill. And if it comes all ready-made — they will take the easy option — it's human nature.

So the important thing is to seek out practitioners or those journalists or those sources of information that have a commitment to trying to sort the truth analyzed and trying to give more objective answers. Really the job of journalism educators is to train students to find such sources because there is no other way, no other way.

Samita Nandy: You are an actor known for a lot of activism — I come across a lot of political issues that you address -all the ethical, social, and political issues in human rights. Do you feel that they are being as effective as you would like them to be — not just yours but social justice movements and your role in them? How do you feel?

Kabir Bedi: One believes in certain causes. I believe in the cause of education, I believe in the cause of helping and preventing blindness. India has one of the largest blind populations in the world. And if something can be prevented, that is the best thing you can do. I am involved in the educational aspects.

I use all the social media that I have to talk about myself as well as promote the causes that interest me.

What I say is disseminated widely enough? Probably not.

But, by the same token, it is proportionate to the amount of time I put into disseminating that news.

Instead of just putting them on Facebook Instagram and Twitter, I can go to all kinds of different forums etc — that I don't do. Because frankly, to make the causes my full-time job, I don't have the time.

And therefore, I just put out there what I believe in, what are the things I hope for. And I hope that those who are following me will take the message forward and carry the message forward.

There are a lot of causes in this world — one can't do all of them — one chooses the ones that they can make a difference.

The ones that I am involved in — I have certainly seen a great difference happened — it has improved fundraising, it has improved the morale of the people in the field — the results are being spectacular.

This is real, tangible change.

When you know that so many thousands of people are saved from blindness because of surgical interventions that happened — that prevented them from going blind — you know you have done good.

The rest is numbers — it doesn't matter if you help 1 person 1000, or 10000 — main thing is the processes.

So one has to work with the reach one has.

But hope that the reach amplifies itself through those people that are part of my reach.

Samita Nandy: And I think what makes it very real and engaging is a lot of the life stories that come along — the contexts in which you write, what you observe in parallel to the causes that you are fighting for. I think that makes it very authentic. Being a living example of change is the most important thing, which Gandhi would say. Bearing witness is something he always advocated for. I believe that every voice counts; every step counts, so to put it out there along with your authentic stories, your contexts — that is very powerful. Because one of the biggest issues that I noticed in tabloid journalism is the loss of the contexts in which a lot of work, whether it is artistic, activist or just educational emerges — so the nuances and subtleties are lost — but I think that's what makes voices very original.

Another issue that I noticed in overall education, art, and activism is that we use a lot of words but it becomes more powerful when you have certain images and real facts along with them. And you use a lot of images. The reason why these images are powerful is that they act as an aesthetic mode of communication — they are not rational; they are not linear. While rationality has really allowed progressive thinking, the same rationality and linear thinking have also made categorization and discrimination possible. According to a TED talk that I watched, artistic modes of inquiries are very important — anything that is sensed, perceived.

What came out of the last conference that I hosted is how fashion can act as an activist tool in pop culture.

We are focusing on popular culture and how tabloid journalism is dealing with it. Fashion, particularly glamorous fashion, is coming into question. Most people have social media profiles; they stylize and re-fashion themselves, re-contextualize themselves. So, in my mind, fashion can act as a political tool to bring change — this is very non-verbal e.g., Bibi Russell what has done.

Kabir Bedi: It is an area of great interest — my wife and I are part of the sustainable fashion movement. They had a number of events in India to promote the fair trade concept, to promote the sustainable fashion —

#WhoMadeMyClothes. And ask those questions and make manufacturers more aware of the possibilities of the efforts. In fact, as a result of those efforts, Mumbai Fashion Week has one section entirely on sustainable fashion. So the message of sustainable fashion is spreading, as it should spread. Because not only are we talking about the ethics of using underpaid labor but also of using products that are more natural. So that is an important movement — more of my wife's area of interest — Parveen Dusanj Bedi's. But I support the concept fully — I go to their events, show my presence. I hope that the message spreads.

Samita Nandy: I feel that the stories around fashion — or even using fabric within fashion as a text to read in fashion — has a strong potential to reach out compared to a lot of rumors, scandals, and gossips — I think there is an alternative space that fashion can enable — I have hope there too.

Kabir Bedi: The real scandal is not who slept with who — the real scandal is when that building collapsed in Bangladesh shows the extent of exploitation in the fashion world — how many big names are involved and how many of those names have become responsive today as a result of that accident and loss of life — so there is a movement and I am sure it will pick up a lot of steam.

Even in Bombay, plastic is banned and people have started using paper bags. It's just a matter of will, a desire to see a slightly different world.

And that's what's happening at all levels — at private levels, at government levels.

The only thing is that we have to get some aspects of the industry that still hold on to the old order — that still wants to be exploitative, that still wants to be polluting, that still wants to be purely driven by profits. And those people will eventually lose their popularity because people's consciousness is moving in a different direction.

Samita Nandy: Just along the question of fashion activism, do you feel that there are limitations along with its potential? What are the limits of fashion activism?

Kabir Bedi: The limits of fashion activism are:

1. there are manufacturers who are not interested in the topic and just want profit

2. there are customers that are frankly not interested in the larger goals — they just want the cheapest clothes they can get.

So as long this alliance between the manufacturer wanting more profit and the consumer wants to lowest cost continues, then that becomes a limitation. However, if it's clear that there is a social trend against that and that social movement makes such manufacturers uncomfortable and unattractive to the customers, these things will change. There are certainly obstacles.

Samita Nandy: Do you feel that universities could help when it comes to fashion activism or just fashion journalism? What kind of role can universities play?

Kabir Bedi: I think universities need to, in addition to imparting the very valuable knowledge that they do, make students in all subjects of the social dimensions of what they propose to do — whether that is journalism, whether that is fashion, whether that is sports, whether that is cinema — there is a social dimension to it too. And there is a social responsibility for promoting a shared good, which is part of the human condition — we must help each other a lot. And if those things are made clear by the educators, they will lead to students who are more enlightened, therefore become better citizens of the world.

Samita Nandy: Do you think more hands-on work, more field work would really help as opposed to just teaching theory?

Kabir Bedi: Fieldwork obviously helps but fieldwork is expensive and it takes a lot of time. The experience is important but even before the experience, the information is the most important. Those that have the sensibility "oh my god, there is this damage to this, my god I didn't think about that and will use that information to improve things in the world, in the society, in the products they use — they will make the biggest difference. But you can't just bank on fieldwork. You have to allow that the information itself is the biggest influencer. Gone are the days when parents were the only source of information "Daddy, why is the sky blue?" and daddy says "sky is blue because of xyz" — that's the answer. They Google it. Google is the biggest parent today, as far as information goes. Parents have other very valuable functions. But one thing is people are not imprisoned by beliefs, dogmas, and circumstances anymore if they do not want to. They have too much reach around them for information, for new directions. And that's why mentoring people to understand what is available is the single most important thing. It's like that old saying, "give a man a fish, you feed him for a day. Teach a man how to fish, teach him how to feed for a lifetime." Teach people what's out there so that they know what's out there because the biggest sin of all is ignorance in today's information age. And that's the job of an educator — to overcome that ignorance whatever form that takes.

Samita Nandy: In giving that information, do you feel that images, telling visual stories would be effective instead of just reading books?

Kabir Bedi: Of course. Stories are always the most effective form as people have seen stories. Cinema has done its share. Today people are aware of 'blood diamonds' because there are films that are made on the subject that has shown this. The fact that people are aware of the Bangladesh tragedy is because people saw pictures of the Bangladesh buildings collapsing and people being pulled out from there. So if things are put in an audio-visual way, it magnifies the impact — there is no question. We are living in an audio-visual world — never forget that part of the world.

Samita Nandy: And in that mentorship, to facilitate new role models is also the responsibility of educators.

Media educators could use storytelling for social change especially when media and educational institutions are limited to specific research agendas and news agendas. The reason why I think that is because a lot of the discrimination I observe is based on looks. When it comes to discrimination or bias against race, gender, species, or age, it's really around looks. And I feel visual storytelling and images in that storytelling would really help. What would be your take on that?

Kabir Bedi: Well, you are absolutely right. That's also the part of the job of educators — that you just don't give people information. You have to enable people to spread that information. You have to make them facilitators. And the best way to make them facilitators is the use of storytelling. People love listening to stories. You can't just give a set of facts that they are not interested in. But you can link them together in a story that is fascinating. You will absorb without realizing it. So one of the great jobs of educators today is to make 'doers' of tomorrow into storytellers.

Samita Nandy: We come from oral history….

Kabir Bedi: Oral history is, of course, is important but now we have the written word, we have audio, we have visual — we have all aspects. Earlier, people used to come to meetings with a few things written on a piece of paper in their agenda. Today, they come with PowerPoint presentations, they come with mini-movies, brilliant slideshows. It's not just the common man — even in the boardrooms, storytelling is a very important device. People love listening to stories. It's one of the oldest things — sitting under a tree and listening to a wise, old man telling stories. And that ability to tell stories is an art. What is storytelling? What is a story? A good story in its essence has conflict — something that must happen when something cannot. The stronger the 'must', the stronger the 'cannot; the stronger 'the story.' This is the way how you put things. So teaching the art of storytelling of how to take information and turn it into a story that people want to see or listen to is an art and that is one of the big jobs of communicators today, and of educators today, and of parents. Teachers. Mentors. We need a world that is full of storytellers.